Fleur Carnivore

Richard Lyons

Richard Lyons (signature)

*Winner of the
2005 Washington Prize*

THE WORD WORKS
WASHINGTON, D.C.

First Edition   First Printing
Fleur Carnivore
Copyright © 2006 by Richard Lyons

Reproduction of any part of this book in any form or by any means, electronic or mechanical, including photocopying, must be with permission in writing from the publisher. Address inquiries to:

The WORD WORKS
PO Box 42164
Washington, DC 20015
editor@wordworksdc.com

Cover art by Hamlett Dobbins: *Untitled (for M.R.M.)* oil on canvas, 54x46", 2003. Image courtesy of the artist and David Lusk Gallery, Memphis.

Book design, typography by Janice Olson.

Printed by Signature Book Printing, Inc.
www.sbpbooks.com

Library of Congress Number: 2005934337
International Standard Book Number: 0-915380-61-7

Acknowledgments

The Alaska Quarterly Review—"Chinese Winter Jasmine at Saint-Jacques Gate," "Two Self-Portraits Trying to Emerge from an Interior," "A Brief Homage to John Coltrane"

American Literary Review—"Song Not for the Orchid but for Knott"

Arts and Letters—"A Study Using White and Black, Number One"

The Black Warrior Review—"To the Tune of *The Last Time I Saw Paris*," "These Continuous Things"

Brilliant Corners—"Snow Falling through Midnight," "Atonal Raindrops in the Flyway, After Cecil Taylor," "Meditations with the Music of Clifford Brown," "Dream Riffs off Oktoc Road," "Sitting at a Desk, Listening to Cherry and Shepp," "A Meditation Departing from Francis Bacon's *Oedipus and the Sphinx after Ingres, 1983*," "Miles from the Sea (Alternate Take)," "Not for the Birds Blues," "Black Expatriate Playing near the Ligurian Sea"

Cimarron Review—"Reincarnation Blues, Crescent City"

Crazyhorse—"White Memory Number One," "White Memory Number Two"

Facture—"Disquietude Stirred by Oracles"

The Gettysburg Review—"Fee-Fi-Fo-Fum (Alternate Take)," "Yes I Can, No You Can't (Endless Takes)," "A Self-Portrait with Lucian Freud and Max Beckmann," "Red Memory Number One," "Red Slaughterhouse Non-Memory Number One," "Self-Portrait Obscured," "Envy, Augury, and the Indigo Bunting," "Meditations Approaching Nazim Hikmet at the Beginning of Summer," "In Memory of Bill Matthews," "Natural History," "Neither Road Taken," "Our Mutant Gazes," "Six Meditations at the Beginning of Winter"

The Indiana Review—"Footnote the Low Sky"

The Iowa Review—"Monolith, West Texas"

The Louisville Review—"The One Red Stone versus the Myriad"

The North American Review—"Attar of Violet & Loneliness," "The Sun"

The Notre Dame Review—"Acts of Privacy"

The Paris Review—"The Blind Man, Twilight Turning Night," "Lunch by the Grand Canal," "A Series of Photos for the Adoption Agency," "Against Endings: Two Studies"

Third Coast—"Language"

Triquarterly—"Ornette Coleman's Yellow Saxophone at Lenox, Death Memories Rising," "Snow Effects"

For their friendships and their advice or help with
these poems, I would like to thank
Ralph Burns, Nancy Eimers, Sascha Feinstein,
Edward Hirsch, Richard Howard, Sally Johnston,
Bill Kerley, Gary Myers, William Olsen, Stanley Plumly,
Emily Stinson, Peter Stitt, David Wojahn, and
Carla Bley, pianist, *Fleur Carnivore*, recorded live, November 1988,
Copenhagen, Denmark.

In memory of my parents Agnes and Charles Lyons

For Leah Giniusz

*Good Fortune's light as a feather,
but who knows how to carry it?*

*Misfortune's heavy as the earth,
but who knows how to elude it?*

*Everything is! It just is! Stop
lording Integrity over people:*

*it's dangerous! It's dangerous
rushing around parsing the earth.*

—**Chuang Tzu**

Table of Contents

A Brief Homage to John Coltrane   10

ONE — *In the absence that followed our first happiness…*

A Study Using White and Black, Number One	12
Self-Portrait Obscured	13
White Memory Number One	14
Sitting at a Desk, Listening to Cherry and Shepp	15
Meditations with the Music of Clifford Brown	17
Two Self-Portraits Trying to Emerge from an Interior	19
Snow Falling through Midnight	21
Snow Effects	22
Lunch by the Grand Canal	23
Monolith, West Texas	24
Ornette Coleman's Yellow Saxophone at Lenox, Death Memories Rising	25
Footnote the Low Sky	27
White Memory Number Two	28
Neither Road Taken	29
The Sun	30

TWO — *Reconsidering the deadliness of the sins…*

Red Slaughterhouse Non-Memory Number One	32
The One Red Stone versus the Myriad	33
Envy, Augury, and the Indigo Bunting	35
Meditations Approaching Nazim Hikmet at the Beginning of Summer	36
Reincarnation Blues, Crescent City	41
Disquietude Stirred by Oracles	43
Six Meditations at the Beginning of Winter	44
Chinese Winter Jasmine at Saint-Jacques Gate	47

Red Memory Number One	48
To the Tune of *The Last Time I Saw Paris*	49
Natural History	52
Acts of Privacy	53
A Self-Portrait with Lucien Freud and Max Beckmann	54

THREE — *Against endings...*

Song Not for the Orchid but for Knott	58
Miles from the Sea (Alternate Take)	59
Not for the Birds Blues	60
Our Mutant Gazes	62
Against Endings: Two Studies	64
In Memory of Bill Matthews	66
A Meditation Departing from Francis Bacon's *Oedipus and the Sphinx after Ingres, 1983*	67
Language	70
Fee-Fi-Fo-Fum (Alternate Take)	71
Yes I Can, No You Can't (Endless Takes)	73
Black Expatriate Playing near the Ligurian Sea	75
Atonal Raindrops in the Flyway, After Cecil Taylor	76
Attar of Violet & Loneliness	78
A Series of Photos for the Adoption Agency	79
The Blind Man, Twilight Turning Night	81
These Continuous Things	82
Dream Riffs off Oktoc Road	84

About the Author	85
About the Washington Prize	86
About the Word Works	87

A Brief Homage to John Coltrane

There's the cardinal's lunatic blow, a few trills falling

with the taste of the trees, then nothing—bravado broken off—
one breath hushed & generously disseminating.

There's no end to what it fabricates of what is lost,
even from a happy childhood. This tremendous tucking in

is the origin of ash, bird, taxidermy's musical scale.
The desires don't wish to fall on anything like a monsoon.

It isn't father-will or mother-wish. The late-night interviewer
finally shut up as the sax player spoke of a series of notes

that, when played, all matter falls away from itself, all the silences
that accompany a roll call surrendering custody of themselves,

the cries, in minor chords, opening fear's wheel, & then.

ONE

*In the absence
that followed our first happiness...*

A Study Using White and Black, Number One

There is a letter in the crash of black two-by-fours.
My name is written in fire.
Thank goodness for the illegible force of water
from a fireman's hose, the black papier-mâché.

A fireman told me the way to do it was to get inside,
even if your chin crawls on the carpet like a worm.
Blow the fire out from the center of the house,
the windows like mouths spewing the fire
that measures as best it can what we felt
when we saw and heard the world was everything
our first happiness isn't.

A police helicopter lifts an injured horse from a ditch.
The horse is sedated.

From a small drugged euphoria that clouds its eyes
its flailing stops
as if it had its head calm in a bucket.

This is the way you imagine yourself being lifted bodily from the earth,
in a haze of clouds that insist they're not a part of you,
the soot of the stomach turned on its side, its appaloosa side,
mottled energy quivering quietly from within.
What if, in the end, nothing happens, and we go on existing
in the absence that followed our first happiness,

a series of white-eyed weed flowers, one by one,
taking up life by the wayside, on the rim of our looking, looking cross
and looking cross-eyed, certain and bewildered at the same time?

There's an insatiable horse in the fenced-off white field—
it crosses the sunset, it runs its teeth along tufts of grass.

Self-Portrait Obscured

What if memory is effaced from the start
when you take on that face that is not your face
to keep your mother from turning away?

For a long time, that face fascinates.
Then your mother finishes the gesture she's started—
the blue drop of milk at her wrist, warm, then cold.
These are odd feelings to ache with, to ache with beginning,
turning away from yourself toward more commodious spaces
which feel like gossip, someone else's suffering, someone else's thrift.

She wasn't harmed, she was just taken away.
It wasn't just. It just was. You stood corrected then,
for what you don't remember, losing your legs a second,
and then the light swept somewhere else.

For a while there is only the river's sound over stones.
Strange futures are yours, probably poorer, given time.

White Memory Number One

It's as if he spied the snowy world
with a winged coat always over his head.

A woman keeps coming to the lit window and looking out.
He's as sure as I am that the brightness within
precludes any positive archival memory.

What if I say the man is approaching a gravestone
at a quarter after midnight, the lilies an armful of phosphorescence
making an embarrassed bouquet of all the private moments
that I am ruining just as I am overseeing their collapse within?

He's remembering the white hood she wore once
when they went sledding. The wind invented white doves.

The wind invents my deadly participation in his arousal,
the old-fashioned way it makes him drop her off without a kiss

and walk as far as the river where he notices white eyes blown open
on the surface of the water, ice floes beneath his posture of surrender,
nothing drastic, more like single blown snowbells in a window.

I'm as sure as I am forty-eight years old on Tuesday
that he shivers with stagefright standing before us descended from him,
a shiver full of the idealist fancies he doesn't want the rap for,
that he knows we'll live our lives by....

If he could hear us talking in the back of the restaurant
he'd consider himself an immortal, shabby yet sufficient,
his life already lore disguising our voices with heavy drink.

Would he fear the man of whom we speak?

Sitting at a Desk, Listening to Cherry and Shepp

Little spheres, little voids, occupy our boundaries. So much
that doesn't threaten conjures fears we can't disdain with jest
or dismiss out of hand. The other day, over a dozen people
gathered outside my neighbor's house spinning red with light.
Then the paramedics rolled out a gurney with an elderly man

willing to let his illness speak for him. As a spectator or cameo,
I was the codicil to a life which unwrote itself in minutes flat,
the scent of gardenia, the green pollen, dust washing across
wherever the crowd had stood. Cherry and Shepp blow riffs
that squiggle off in the margins like spermatozoa, or shrapnel,

or other ineffable means of saying there really is no edge and
that time doesn't end, unless, as Davis told Coltrane, you take
the instrument out of your mouth. That's not exactly it. Time's
larger than human confection, work's spittle in the mouthpiece.
It's not so easy, my apocalyptic friends, to shimmy your part

onto something higher, more monolithic. The dragon at the gate
is, by most accounts, an up-and-coming sideman. What he does
inside his mouth, his embouchure, produces a sound that braces
the side of the world the way a flying buttress braces a cathedral—
the wind sifting through pines, a chevron's shadow passing fast.

After a number of years, we require less sophisticated calibrations
to corroborate our lonelinesses, less and less spindrift to wade in
to get in over our heads, or at least to hear the world's fluted calls
from a muffled distance, as if ears, like fins, swam under water
so the emotion in muted Gregorian voices might counterfeit hope

even if sometimes they're whispered across a dark cedar swamp,
riding brittle canes articulate with birds, the way a pocket cornet
playing high—almost dog-whistle pitched—kidnaps your attention
to an indifference that isn't harsh, really, just off at some point,
desiring not a thing except not to be interrupted from this dream

emptied of dreams, no phantasmagoria, no contrived raving plot. Imagine bright sun, a stretch of sand, the scent of sea and salt rising from beneath, holes breathing, ragged weeds struggling from sand mounds, no sense of self body-Englished in, no dock, no boats coming swiftly and softly toward you with the sun.

Meditations with the Music of Clifford Brown

     1.

Fatigue and failure, believe me, take up space at the edges
where the mind pushes these, the way wind pushes clouds
just off-shore where coral lies beneath, crippled with syntax,
letting all the voices rise like inhibitions we wish to excavate
with the searchlights piercing the black territories of the sea.

It's the field not the detail, it's the field that holds things fast,
crumbled glass and witch hazel, a field of vision razed by vision.
A man blows a trumpet, two-thirds of his lip in the mouthpiece.
Vision recedes behind perspective like an ancient amphitheater,
all the mis-listenings as numerous as weeds, bristling mercies.

     2.

A man inflates his cheeks, and the sound through the bell
swells embedded sensations not held in check so much
as allowed to prowl just there, unnamed, before going down
with an exalted dip beneath the surface I've grown used to,
a practiced grief ready to inflate the red balloon of the heart.

The skin awakens memory, numinous clouds of fog rising,
the muscles riding swollen with blood and undulating algae.
The past is part of how we step out from it and haven't yet
in each new step. That's why separate memories seem contrived,
dressed up with betrayal, and what I said I was in years gone
is just that, too gone to say, as if the instant could hold anything.

My memory is a rough stretch of sand, sand dollars embedded
above a sandy cache of eggs, but, otherwise, the field of vision
is incorruptible. The wind is high, wound-up with machinations
of blowing a path straight through instead of pockmarking the view
with stories in which someone is trying to take it easy on himself.
The wind is high and nothing flies except an engine's high whine.

3.
The salt houses are puffed-up paper lives, isolate seaside lives,
the lungs hyperventilating in such a confined space they are small
blue blossom-spikes at noon and dusk, open and closed at once,
the way the waves pretend to break on the rocks. The human eye

blinks to lubricate itself with tears. Brownie is playing the trumpet,
the sound blasting the decorum of the dead. That's the way
the dead like it, deadly quiet, after the volcanic self has blown its top,
and what it was back then spews so high the clouds curl with ash,
noodles of smoke dissipate to the very edge of everything. One

of me is peaceful, lying among the squash tendrils, the flowers
almost heart-shaped, pulsating at my ear. One of me can't prevent
the instrument from blazing lies through aching eardrum tissue.
I have fantasies of hurting people, hurting what spawns these.
The horsepower clops hooves of wet sand—the ocean recedes.

4.
Panting spirals and trills, Brownie blows each note its signature.
The ones he'll never lip are elegy enough, ripples in my wrists,
one long breath like a banner whooshed out the back of a jet.
What he gives the air to memorize he'll immediately wish back.
He's floating like straw among those bereft of swing, of smokes,
bereft of an old black shoe marking time. The quiet holding still.

Each half-cup of sound empties a plea for mercy, a noisy plea.
A yellow crucifix screeches itself through the trumpet's bell.
I want to drop my arms limp beneath its rise, a deposition,
but I'm not the Son of Man. I'm not Brownie blowing wails.
My memory is a blank stretch of sand, sand dollars embedded
above a turtle's nest. The tentativeness swings: short puffs,
images wiped from the field by a force neither in nor out, a whole
engendered whole, the opaque autobiographical burning whole.

Two Self-Portraits Trying to Emerge from an Interior

1.

Cheek and jowl are a winestained birthmark
in the shape of a telephone receiver that the rest of the face
doesn't want to hear from.
Because the wide-screen TV is black, the face stares out from itself,
the features straining like greyhounds against their leashes.

The eyes vertigo like bruised thumbs toward what's to see.
The dresser's photograph refuses light and so is black,
a black that isn't the absence of subject but its intensification,
a sheen that ripples from within like the sea at night,
though the subject is nowhere near the sea.

There is no doubt that happiness is sometimes black,
a sea of happiness when delusions are shaken out, then stuck with pins
to the dry winter night rippling the curve of fabric and stitch
so that they almost let go, that is,
when the self lets the attention rove like a lantern across the black exact
edge of rock, the fabric and stitch of nowhere near.

2.

The hardwood floor drops in lines from where you're perched
on one of those chairs made from a vine
convinced by constant pressure to grow in the shape of a chair:
a few loops with a wicker bottom, the kind with which the lion tamer
fends off the lion, the flesh of his face rippling from a roar we can't hear.
We're hearing it, the eardrums tingling at the back of the throat.

In chimpanzees that wage war, the males have evolved larger than the
        females.
They rove in gangs on the periphery where the grass is beaten down.
In the afternoon beneath the trees, these males grow quiet.

Their eyelids cease trembling.
R.E.M. is granted only to species who have little fear of attack,
who do not sleep like cream on the top of coffee, not like cats
that only appear to be sleeping all the time
on the tops of washers, at the ends of beds.

There is an actual cat, mottled cat, curled on the daybed.
In the foreground a few sheets of newspaper have lain so long
we can make out the grooves from the hardwood floor,
we can make out the news alphabet feeding on itself.
The chair is twisted at such an angle you could never really sit
    comfortably.
Is that the idea? Are those buff-colored bowlers hung on the wall by the
    door
or are they trophy heads from a safari in Botswana?

The Polar bear rug has been removed: how else would the world floor
look so good, so dust free? No wonder your face defies physiognomy.
No wonder your features won't sit still long enough so we can recognize
what we are looking at as portrait, as self-portrait, as self-portrait
    obscured.

Snow Falling through Midnight

What each cone of light from the lampposts collects
isn't the ice underfoot impeding progress as you speed ahead
and isn't the deliberate minuscule slit in & out of the white,
the moment of forgetting before it's forgetfulness.

Maybe it's a nest for invisible birds, a nest of white sticks,
strips of paper, dead white leaves, for all the good
a configuration is, deserted, white. Open your loss.

Most of the seeing—years back—was sucked through into its opposite
where there isn't a face, where desire in desiring affixes one,
the snowflakes lengthening into the flexible lines of light
as desire wind-swirls them up and away from the eyes that view them.

They flee between the birth star and the mothering exponential space
that leaves a little chaos in each creation, how in a hot jazz session,
certain instruments lay a field of white that is so full of sound
it is soundless—and certainly without this, the score couldn't ever
be heard right, that is, in the way the swing is meant to be heard

when the swinging hears it, which is in movement away from it,
the space through which the white is moving,
the fleck after fleck you can't control but which depends on you,
at least in part, the wrist's resisting, the superstitious hand and wrist,
all those individual ancestral flecks spoken into an abyss
that masquerades as a large body of water in the midst of a storm—
sounds meant for life's fire, time's wind,
all your cousin words, sibling rats nibbling from underneath
the granary that is your dead mother, all her desires to sustain you.

Snow Effects

(German Alps, 1980)

Some complain how time drags itself and then accelerates.
Some admit, as everyone will, that the past can't be changed,
except to lie, deceive someone concerning the effects of memory,
vertical shadows to misapprehend what this stranger in down
is doing as he climbs a snowy incline with a bag of groceries
as if a ghost, reeling in its extinction, had turned white
to see how it feels to be included in what's around it.
A brook that looks like an arm bubbles down, freezing
a second before it resumes its descent into a family of trees
all bent one way from the winds off the steppe.

Back up at the top of the town, the pellets continue falling fast,
and the plows—stripped to their motors—look like racing cars
with parachutes billowing out behind them,
the way the wind together with the snow
accompanies him everywhere, cold fire, cold earth, ice.

No matter how fast the plow plows, then or now, the past
drifts into featurelessness. Wasn't memory a blank from the start,
a mother like a white wind sweeping through an open door
so that any venture, any going-away in a too-small pair of boots,
is a freefall through the architecture of a woman's body,
the architecture of snow, nervous because its bearing is nervous,
an avalanche of interiors like bees munching plaster of Paris?
Each alpine house pinches its white nomenclature of ash.
A snowy ash, a lethal ash, sifts through the roof of the world.

Lunch by the Grand Canal

Harry Donaghy, an ex-priest, is telling us
that, after ten rounds, the welterweight was still panting
from a literal hole in his heart.
The fish the waiter lays before me on a white plate
is hissing through its eye, I swear it.
Harry spills out a carton of old photos
between the bread & the vials of vinegar.
The people in the pictures are friends of his aunt, whose body

he's signed for & released, now on a jet lifting from Rome.
He says he's always preferred Venice.
Here, a Bridge of Sighs separates this life from the next.
One of the photos, he thinks, is of his aunt.
She's no longer young, having dropped a cotton dress at her feet

so the artist at arm's length might see her beauty
as if it had already slipped away. Across from me,
Paige Bloodworth is wearing a red hat, which looks good on her,
but she hasn't said a word, so pissed we missed the launch
to San Michele where Pound is buried.

For her, Harry's unidentified relatives
posing on the steps down to the Grand Canal
are lifting stones from their pockets
and pelting the poet's coffin as it eases out
on a black boat, chrysanthemums hoarding their perfumes.

I'm stroking the curved prow of a boat as if it were
the neck of a wild stallion rearing close
for a hidden cube of sugar or a slice of apple.
Miss Bloodworth's hat becomes a figure in memory's contract
as it lifts over water the color of tourmaline.
Harry's big hands trap all the photos, spilling the wine.
It's the winter of 1980, just warm enough
to sit outside as I remember. The rest of that year
no doubt is a lie.

Monolith, West Texas

Peach on the dash, meaty compass I taste to the pit-stone,
I barely reach for you
               the way, off-stage, an actor in black
hesitates as if his mother's room were always there before him.

Before me, the white sky like a shade stretches to the horizon,
the ruby fruit of the cholla electric with messages.

Six miles away, El Capitan, an austere piece of jade,
pins down the bewildered edge of Texas.

I want to say my seeing has placed it there
                          like a jar in Tennessee,
but it's not tamed much, nothing in its dominion, the seam of my coat
a fat kiss, my body as luminous as a tortured soul in a da Vinci
rising & falling through apparitions of itself.

Ornette Coleman's Yellow Saxophone at Lenox, Death Memories Rising

This music allows the independent units of the rhythm section more salience
if salience might be shared, a drum's errant firing, the hi-hat
flying off the handle, or nearly so, offering a detour the horn will refuse,
or take when it damn well pleases as long as the twists and turns
are worth the ride, the bassist swaying the contrabass on its spear.

Compare this with Breughel's pasture-wide fandango. Identity
is a free-ranging guinea fowl, all the rich verdigris and blue flecks,
yellow streaks and spindly red dots. The gods have clipped its wings
so the industrious male works off and on to erect a secret bower,
the minarets of straw grounded with the slick spoor of certain rats.

Then the trumpet or cornet gets in on the act, and the warp and woof
grow even more complicated. Listen to the mist in the thicket.
This music slashes the way wild pigs submerge themselves in shadows
so black the sun can't touch them. This music competes over misery.
This music wants you to appreciate the ground you're standing on
when everything in sight seems on fire, certainly no worse than

the malarial way one might die, cheesecloth draped over your face,
while the damaged little ones wonder how the demons hidden in the dust
of the blood might emerge, if not now, someday, if not then, when exactly?
Why can't anyone say for sure what it is we have to get off our chests?

Sipping glasses of ginger ale, the mourners seem giddy. Then the nurse
    comes in
and the family turns serious, like pinching off the tip of a balloon you've
    just inflated,
almost hyperventilating. Do your lungs ache? Can't say. Really. Then she
    takes
the bedpan out to the rest of the neighborhood, fireworks too early for the
    holiday.

It's more likely this music has something to do with feelings you've
> experienced
emerging from a sickroom, or sneaking out of the funeral home while
> everyone else,
certainly braver than you, hovers over the dead countenance that's more
> than likely
responsible for how little air there is to breathe in there. The all-ending
> changes.

You remember your sister's face crumbling as the funeral director had
> trouble
removing your dead mother's rings. But that, as they say, is a different story.
The way the bass chides the saxophone you'd think this music has to
> depart,
dropping sadness in the rush, the way a cartoon rocket fizzes out and flops
so you won't miss it or its chimp astronaut chatter-flashing its crooked
> teeth.

Certainly the yellow sax's got the chops to send its breath out beyond the
> stars,
but the pitch slashes out, snaking a noose around the red-faced elated moon,
that poor medallion burdened with the wishes of a girl who finds herself
> lost,
betrothed to the accomplished fellow off riding a horse in the annual
> competition.
He'll be back after dark when this band has dispersed, when the air has
> cleared.
But, for now, intensity is its own aesthetic, and the moon burns your lap.

Footnote the Low Sky

Of course the fascination with trains has something of death in it,
an acrid sense of letting go—
not for those who climb the cars as they always have
in the dark before dawn when the cars move slowly in their sleep,

after the railroad dicks and shiftbosses
stumble through their rounds in the switching yard.

Gary tells me the body he found in an open car
in the dark before dawn was cold meat.
The yard boss let it through to save the paperwork:
just a bum, a tramp, a hobo, a nobody with too many names.

Somebody else tells me the caboose is "a thing of the past."
An end car shows up when it will, when it does, like the future.

Just when the eye becomes entranced, there's no train there,
only the crossing lights blinking against a low sky.
I know a little about low skies, about "the line that eats and digests scribbles."

Footnote the painter Paul Klee. The past is still happening in the future.
Klee writes this, and I believe it as I believe that passing is not to die
but to inhabit nowhere without feeling bad about it. Footnote the low sky.

We all know how, in German, the nouns couple like asylum mates
afraid of the nothing that is before the eyes,
a locomotive in a thick tasteless soup, a low sky in a man's bed.

Dear stranger, dear self, just when did you become the world archive,
when you ran you dead mother's necklace through your hands?

You're less now than ever before. The dead hiss this. I whisper this.
The train's passing, blue-ventilated cars empty of cows.

White Memory Number Two

I'm nothing original standing beneath the sworded damsel
on the Arch of Triumph,

remembering my father's harangue against the citizens,
saving their asses, twice, damn frogs,
the past ahead of my every step. He doesn't like the wine,
tearing a roll of hard bread with his teeth,

he who didn't get to walk in the fire, the family lore
of can-can girls and cabarets when the only photos

are black-and-whites in England, some trees, my father
stuffing one hand inside a baseball glove. The ball

is a long time returning from the other side of an English meadow,
from his fellow survivor, who died the other day
showing his granddaughter how to eat ice cream at a mall.

The mall should remain nameless, the English meadow.
This is a way of keeping the future from dissolving away.

At times, he concentrates on the archival ache in his head.
Someone's broken in and poured acid over the film, men
trained in chemical weapons, tossing a baseball back and forth
among some identifiably English trees, limey trees, stoic acorns.

Everything about this past declares thrift, standing very still
in a meadow soaked with sunshine & waiting,

waiting to be called to action. The afternoon sun is permanent
as if history had unfurled its tailor's tape measure as far as it could go.

Neither Road Taken

A bright car pulled up where I was walking,
the driver leaning over. I didn't hear his questions,

my arms gesticulated some configuration of streets.

It was winter & ice hung in the branches like a thousand lost
sewing needles descending through the fabric of the afternoon.

It was spring & everything was imminence.
It was summer & the clouds swiftly passed over our heated element.

I told the man I was born beneath the wooden trestle of a train,
that loud noises captured my attention,

not the lefts & rights of destination.

Bearing the white needlepoint of a scar at the base of my neck,
I told him the road to the right was covered in hyacinth,

the one to the left dropped down along the aqueduct to hell.
Choose the oldest, I said to him, choose the oldest.

The Sun

Water, through clay, on the back of my hand,
I tuck the shroud around the face,
the face itself a kind of child, a face

composed of all the expressions that ever crossed it.
They're closed away within now
and that's just as well, a million raw originals
not meant to be recalled.

So much must be willingly given up
if you want to remember even the lines
around your mother's thin lips.
We can never properly lose the sun.

TWO

*Reconsidering
the deadliness of sins...*

Red Slaughterhouse Non-Memory Number One

My father is wearing a raincoat, lofting an umbrella.
He's wearing a priest's collar, white tab at the trachea.
It looks as if he's hearing the moon's confession.

The moon is the long red jacket of Angus.
I wish I were making this up.

It may be the stirring in the room where my father is standing.
The walls are infinitely extendable with these red flags of meat.

The carcasses are singing like fervent parishioners.
I sense somehow that this song is watching me
so everything's coated with self-consciousness.
I could do worse, one could do awfully worse.

There are bloody penances on the umbrella.
The song is cold, literally, a cold prayer.

My father wants less than shame for me.
He wants me to be comfortable with the approved cuts of meat.
He wants me to approve of the moon hacked by butchers
so swift and expert the sinews don't feel themselves loosening.

With the umbrella, he walks past me hanging on a hook with the moon.

The moon is in remission from the time before time, the time before shame,
the period of time a good poet called the shape of an angel,
nights without shame, moonless nights,
nights before my face dissolved with shame,

the very first shape ashamed of itself,
the vaguely luminous time shunted by these very words.

The One Red Stone versus the Myriad

The One Red Stone vies with the ten thousand things,
what the Chinese call everything outside the mind,
including the ten thousand things inside it—
call it the birth of mayflies, the myriad feasting on our world
that, by design, is meant to deceive us, meant to feast us.

Entry for November 2: "Vague hope, vague confidence."
For Kafka, this measures a certain amount of progress.
For me there's this: before the quiet in the trees
lifts through the impoverishment a sparrow
contortedly humming its dark wings, you are dead.
In the half-bath, your head against the door,
You don't want us to find you, blood on the lip.
You are afraid, like me, to owe anyone anything.

Can the body twist like that, the cheek a roseate beef?
Your head drops, unsupported by the neck.
The privacy of the act curls up like a child
when the weight pours in from the obscured stars.

Contempt is how I tamp down the teeming forms
that scare me, all the forms of flint and fire that scare me.
I pay no homage unless fear is a kind of homage.
The present is a weak form of praise.
There's no actual spot to speak from.
Whose voices are these, washing over me their noisy lotions?

I walk the river named for you, dip beneath the bridges
through the odor of oxidized iron, fiercely red,
which can be inside us too. Death inside us, Franz knew.
The asylum grounds are a weak form that can't hold me.
The nurses hurry by—their torsos like the hands of clocks,
their soft, good-on-the-heels rubber shoes. Tick. Tock.

When I was young and agitated with an enlarged heart,
a nurse would bring a paper cup with the juice of an apple
squeezed into it, her hand against my cheek in the hospital dark.
It was love and it was shock, that hand, a kindness from the dark.

In a mist, mayflies eyespot images of themselves
the way the mind sometimes fears itself, stares at itself....
All of life shakes its wings on the surface of the illuminated pool,
a yellowish benevolent light.
I must not talk with the dead—it is false, it is forbidden;
it is not, it is not—their living forms can swallow any one of us.

Envy, Augury, and the Indigo Bunting

I envy how the sky surrounds itself without blocking the view.
I envy the sleeve that cuts the middle of a woman's palm.

I envy a man with glasses and how those glasses fear everything I say.
I envy the man hiding in Bangkok.

I envy the boy who clings to his father's side
as if my words wiped this man like a figure from the slate at school.

I envy the man who sleeps in his dead mother's undersize bed.
I envy the bunting's rare appearance on the ground.

Down invisible rivulets, down the surrounding slopes,
the rain envies its way to standing water where the bunting drinks,

envying the next flit its motor function hasn't even flitted yet.
I envy the bird watcher spying every tilt of the wing.

I envy the young man's effeminate gesture, how it doesn't hurt
when he breathes, when he touches his wrist with the index finger.

I fear the entrails of the bunting into which the whole world stares.
I fear the hollow leg bones clicking in the old woman's palm.

The future never is, it dies to arrive. *I'm not what you said I'd be*,
the future whispers. The future is…. Use any other way to speak

besides words, the sage reminds me, extract envy like a molar
that's tied to a slamming door. Envy deadens the capillaries

that surround the mouth so, sometimes, when I talk, I know
that what I've just said is dead and floating menacingly free.

Meditations Approaching Nazim Hikmet at the Beginning of Summer

> *"You sound like a poet."*
> *"Yes, unfortunately.*
> *And when poetry gets mixed up in this business,*
> *it's all the more disgusting…"*
> — Human Landscapes

(Mid-June, Noon)

If the mayfly is as tasty as an imploding star,
then the nestlings will, in time, sing their own anthem

and prove sustenance the beginning of eloquence.
But the mystic advises: as spring passes, shut your mouth.

The six senses use us, noon a gooseneck lamp rousing secrets.
From across the plaza, a woman counts the ticks of the bomb

affixed to the ignition of the red sedan
that two well-dressed men are climbing into.

The black thickens her brother's beard beneath the palms
in the dirty courtyard, where he lies, where she buried him.

The bastards chopped off both his hands.
A note pinned to the body quipped: can't carry a tune.

"Now," she whispers, the explosion ripping their very seeds,
their balls in their laps—a sick, twice-told joke.

The spray of glass an echo.
Are they laughing now in their spit & blood?

(Mid-June, Sunset)

One of the guards has bitten off one of your nipples
and busted two of your teeth.

Solitude can be poisonous, swallows circling the mosque.
A prayer to Allah is broadcast at every corner.

No one will believe He spoke to you, a prisoner
soaking right through your tunic.

Nazim, I am your solitude, a dry soot.
Make no excuses, breathe with the center of your body, like a bird.

Your release papers arrive on a Friday.
The guard pats you on the cheek.

"Watch yourself, old camel."

(Mid-June, Dawn)

A bird cries from somewhere off the alley.

One chickpea on the sill is a sign they're watching.
The sun's wing tries the lashing.

You're trying to dream of your mother mushing chickpeas
with two large cloves of garlic. Her voice a bird's.

No, her actual voice was dogged & demanding,
more like a spatula to chickpeas

if chickpeas had ears!

(Mid-June, Twilight)

            Elegance must seem accidental,
else it traps us in its knowledge of the past,

time itself trapped as I imagine the black liquid
spilling from a samovar that surely, sitting on a ledge

in a courtyard in Ankara, has a guttural sound to denote it.
Memory is eternal, Roman & Ottoman aqueducts

still crumbling beneath the streets.

                       I live where elegance is suspect,
where very little collapses into ruins before it's swept aside

like letters deleted on a speedy PC saying, no,
there is a more perfect way to say this now, isn't there?

I sprinkle salt & pepper on both sides of the red mullet
lacquered in olive oil & herbs. In the lengthening shadows

the hydrangeas glow like clusters of chipped Christmas bulbs.
The short frequent dive-bombings above the lawn

are marked by a diminution that grows as the light goes.
A male's dazzlingly iridescent head pants in the heat

as if to confirm that equanimity is a form of surrender
the way a woman in Ankara might feel it, seeing a swallow

spill through the air, green-tiled mosque in the distance,
the sun refusing its downward arc a little longer.

(————)

May our voices tremble the annals of the air like Ataturk's,
the soot a recalcitrant ink.

Don't bet on it. I pin you with this cynical cut,
hearing only the voice in my head counting the dead.

The swallows dive toward the olive trees.
Make no excuses, breathe with the center of your body, like a bird.

A bird's life is nothing to envy, that's what you wrote.
The flying insects are asterisks. Nazim, I wouldn't give

a wet shovel for your miserable life. A fighter plane dives low
over the houses, shadows smudging you with thumbs.

(————)

You remember a swallow circling high in the air,
but you can't say for sure from what spot you were looking

or whether the looking mattered as you stared,
a praying wall between you & the general ignorance,

what words may never join, at best, part calculation, part chance,
what revolves inside the body part calculation, part chance.

Your face doesn't lie; it hurts a little but doesn't humiliate.
The Asian-looking boy you passed a crust of bread to gobbles it.

There's nothing private each time a swallow dives behind a mosque.
As you pull down your prison pants, the boy is watching

as if the trail darkening the wall describes the trajectory of a bird.
Make no excuses, breathe with the center of your body, like a bird.

Inside solitude, like an unripe fig, is a white joyous truth.
My death isn't there. I carry it in my shirt pocket, little bomb.

In someone's good time, our voices will sweep the mottled wall.
They won't unite us, Nazim, who leave behind these words.

Reincarnation Blues, Crescent City

You're walking beneath a hot sun, a lighting store's dark interior
a dapple of branches and recesses. Then, a delible whirling page
from the mind's border, halted as with the horn of a fingernail,
forces a glimpse: the way the vendor is holding your shoulder
haggling must be a sport, a hat lifting in gradations of shadow,
two friends angling out of the frame of memory's deceptive lens,
almost free....

Then you're back in the present, alone, humming the sped-up bass
to a hard-bop version of "Three Blind Mice," the nursery rhyme
bled out of it, the housecleaners having thrown the towel in,
the scent of Murphy Soap lingering a moment
before things begin to smell pretty much as they've always smelled,
sun motes and the fray of grass, the future as dirty as the past,
the past gone enough for you to enjoy it accelerating back
into gone for good. No, it's another day's misfiling
ready to fire out again when least appreciated....

To look at the passing itself takes a lifetime's attention,
the way Curtis Fuller hook-fingers his slide to the vibrato
hemming from the bell, the bass trying to play it quiet,
the way a bird, an eye-fleck, blends with the bark, then departs,
a quiver of what was or what might have been, delusion's ruse,
the corrosive sway of time. Everything can be transformed,
deformed, and obliterated with light, that's what Man Ray insists.
In one of his rayographs, black pellets float in front of a breast,
its sphere in soft focus, barely visible, the erect nipple
this side of nearsightedness, the eye's vindictive glare.

So you drove all night through Illinois, heading south,
climbing out at 2 a.m. to relieve yourself in the high grass.
You learned the blue chicory refuses to be pulled from the earth.
You want to be resilient like that, like the chicory, not craving
any special ground, not craving the nickel sweat of names.
So you drove all night through Mississippi, heading south.

Will you be found wanting in the end if the wanting never ends,
if the eyelid suddenly lifts, a life span's looking too modest
to crowd the frame of today's fleeting script as darkness lifts
off the continent's edge and a torch singer drops her voice,
sobbing for us, "for us all" not precise since the past recedes,
okay, backs away, whatever turn of phrase will calm you down,
let you fall back stumbling, let the approximate dirt eat your dead.

You wanted to know all that they said you weren't allowed to know
and, since they loved you and they were dead, they let you fall,
discovering in earth's crust a fire so hot rock grows. A man must pass
through the eye of the needle, the priest said, the camel's hinds
slipping a man's baggage before he can enter and be safe....
But what about the bundles unraveling, blowing away in sand,
waylaid by scoundrels who serve no one? Don't these scriptures
confirm the individual's loneliness, a person apart from the world
from which he's made, sand and ashes, papers and names?

Charlie Byrd was picking "How Insensitive" with such dexterity
you'd have thought he wrote it. As he autographed the sleeve,
he seemed old and tired, but pleased that anyone liked his fingerwork.
You shifted your weight as he retraced the letters of his name.

More to the point is Buddy Bolden's literally blowing his horn
as if returning along Decatur from his own Dixie dirge.
In the lockdown, one guy plays his feces like a xylophone.
Another—hang-mouth—bangs his kneecap like a snare.
It's all in how you stuff the beast's mouth, playing the changes.
Take, for example, the manic boy drumming so hard the hi-hat flies,
a kid skinny enough to drop his heft through a slingshot,
death's penury rended by the peal of a cornet, love and hate
intemperate as pigs in corn, the embalming fluid a hot tisane,
Ray Charles and Elvin Jones high-fiving it in the foyer,
all the forgotten mammas and sickly johns, the tripe and the trickle,
the self-righteous and the insane, the torturers, the choir boys,
the contrabass and its swollen belly, a man's embouchure
on the world's pink tip, too much to bear, too much, more.

Disquietude Stirred by Oracles

                        The ill man braids his hair
to match the entrails' blue augury. The snake's finite loop.

The lazy man loves his own face, its future.
The healthy man is small, almost modest, unrestrained.

He breathes the way the giant oak breathes, all at once.
Thrown wide with insects, the oak falls into itself.

Lightning has cut a V in the thick crown of the tree.
Each day a bitter gall drops, a branch disengages.

What is there to say? The master Chuang Tzu has said as much
on the virtues of uselessness. At least it isn't protective.

The oak is sand, indecipherable hieroglyphics lifting in wind.
Sin was invented by those who rule with a sort of lazy greed.

Beyond the vanishing point, barbarians tie up sand-colored tents.
Shaggy palms sway from roots sipping at the heart of the earth.

Even the lazy can smell the saffron toasted golden over fires.
The lazy have violent dreams. They fire carbines into the night.

Beyond the oak, the lazy say, there's nothing to squabble about.
Beyond the oak, the lazy say, there's no profit in sifting sand.

Long after the larynx has let go its lyre-strings & chime,
language will foliate leaf by leaf, axil by axil, seed by seed.

The master Chuang Tzu has said as much about uselessness.
The healthy man is small, almost modest, unrestrained.

Six Meditations at the Beginning of Winter

Is this gratitude, everything the sun replaces—
the light cut by nine meadowlark pines?

Match-flame blue bean blossoms ignite in rows.
Everything is that which we've been meaning to say.

The trouble is we're always beginning,
no matter what the sin-counters crave.

From the heels of my hands to the heels of my thorny feet,
the musculature of syntax stretches—

the palms of my hands, no stigmata, two little pis-tol-a suns.
A perfected breathes all the way to his heels.

Out of the bloody sky, self-loathing & self-love
carve our blue anatomies.

———•———

Just when our circumlocutions are about to cease,
the wind whips dead leaves up in circles.

Behind glass at the corner, sea oats bluer than iris
stick up through the hole in a child's globe.

When everything else is stripped, when, for a second,
we cease our song, the sleeves of our hands

like rare white roses will telegraph their scent.
A perfected breathes all the way to his heels.

Two plain-capped starthroats, those insects of the bird world,
target the pendulum-swinging red nectar.

There will be a dull joy as we articulate each other's names.

———•———

Among the little tags where blue heron tulips will come,
a man in baggy shirt & pants heaves a sundial,

the sun shadowing down the west. Should it be elsewhere?
Our first flesh is good so we are, by nature, ourselves.

When Voltaire wrote cultivate your own garden,
he meant each of us has to get his house in order,

he meant each of us must remain each,
a tulip bulb in the black earth of its blossoming.

The man sits against the trunk of a tree, tips his head back,
the exhausted constellation *so small it has no within*.

What we will have for each other in the end is our bodies.
Should the orchids of our hands break a roll of bread?

They are correct, there's the moon on the right, the sun on the left.
A shark's fin shadows down the west.

———•———

After a go at prayer beads & the soot of candles,
in baggy shirt & pants, I go out with a bottle & three glasses,

line them up on the low fence & pour cheap merlot
in honor of Li Po, the T'ang Dynasty's second great poet.

Then, from thirty paces, I fling white garden stones
at this gallery, the stones hushing in the brush.

The cobalt blue stems in the last rays of sunlight
are midspring's grape hyacinth, the sentinel muscari.

My shoes lolling their tongues like Attila bulbs
unearthed at the beginning of winter,

I dandle each wisdom that ages my body—
O, let none of us dissolve, let none of us dissolve.

When the Yellow Emperor ascended on a dragon,
the few, clinging to its beard & claws, flung to the dust & rocks,

never got over their injuries, nor died, each limb a phantom pain,
a cinnabar cloud of inspecifics, as if the red dust that never matters

were all we had. One noon, out walking among the trajectories,
I came upon a covered bridge, the old cedar dry with sun.

I stood inside, both ends broiling with light.
The yellow slats between my feet

broke any idea of things-other-than-the-self—
the vertebrae's vibrating harp.

Midnight flat tire—within earshot, the western sea.

Above tire iron & jack, a stick of sulphur.
It burns like the ash tulip, death's flora, body plural & percussive.

Stranger, unclasp the brass knuckles of your name,

dissolve into the horizon garment of no memory,
feel your lungs lift, murmurings, the heart's fist.

Chinese Winter Jasmine at Saint-Jacques Gate

The least doesn't rend the sky with a blast—
it eats its winter grief, a crabapple pinched to smoke.

      Our tough yellow blossoms have no need for bodies,

each one of us re-formed with the exact same face.
Without any leaves, our faces sink into themselves.

      December light (the sun's wings) shrinks to ash.

Where are yesterday's snows? Poor thief, poor thief.
Poor thief. The least doesn't rend the sky with a blast—

      one of the blackbirds lifts off a limb to light on the next,

tethered by its iridescence to a blood-tinctured sky.
Each then uncounts itself: crow, grackle, raven, snow.

      My eyes won't close, my voice the wind's dark name.

Don't tell me the heavens trouble the face of the earth.
There's nothing angrier than the black water rising in me.

Red Memory Number One

Nothing is real in a past you tinker with so much
it's as unknowable as what's ahead,
a system of streets all converging in a star at your feet.

Driving the thoroughfare, you describe turrets and cul-de-sacs,
moldings shaped like animals, the small inert fruit trees.

A break in the skyline allows you to see the river,
sunlight on the water making you think of red ice, red winter.

There was fire in the distance, controlled fire, in barrels
burning red-hot light. You couldn't work by this distant light,
but it was the little bearing the evening was willing to grant you
as you lifted the sacks Dad wanted put up in the icehouse.

The past is your father, the late hour masquerading as your father.
Humming a song somehow behind it all, you made sure
everything was right, rearranging bags you had heaved onto the floor.
In the exhaustion you imagined pigs doped inert for shipping.

You wondered why they didn't moan as you loaded them.
The cold had chapped your face by then,
so you invited the little piggies to occupy your red face,
suckle its red loneliness. You invited your father's tone of voice

to see if you could, to see if you could stand it, to berate the pigs
for witnessing the wrathful panic of your father's towering there
to verify that you weren't up to the task, didn't respect
the same things your father did, like red winter and stoic quiet.

The sky was red with suffering, which you were sure
was more than just your own selfish view of things.

To the Tune of *The Last Time I Saw Paris*

Clarity has always been a problem, the way the light banks itself
among buildings with stone lions flanking the stairs, light inside the
    feeling

that we're truly suspended inside a feeling that is falseness
raised exponentially, the way cathedral arches dim in increments the
    interior light,

the way a skinny woman leaning against the lion's head, rubbing her foot,
is a tired pause in a journey that, by definition, must exclude all
    onlookers,

onlookers looking on anyhow & not understanding much of anything
except the pleasurable trajectories of light cut by shadows,

which isn't enough, though of course we look a long time.
New norms, like old ones, should be destroyed. This is how the stone
    shadows operate,

squares we cross as if they were ours alone, a loneliness shared &
    therefore intensified,
the way a love cry from the next room of the Hotel Parthenon

still dissolves your very listening existence on the other side of the wall,
all the gathering of the winged buttresses in the neighborhoods

surrounding your very notion of individual breath, the way the blackbirds
descending the gray-green falling day are a curtain pulled around a bed

where you lie dying, comforting those close to you. If every leaf falls,
do you see yourself sitting in a confessional beneath the bare trees,

fingering penances? When it comes right down to it, you don't want to
 punish anyone
though, in your dreams, a woman you know is carrying an anvil

from the trunk of her car into the basement of an administration building.
She carries it like a burden she would kill to keep, like a chunk of divine
 light,

an anvil of heavy light, heavy water, from the trunk of her car down a ramp
into the basement of an administration building. You don't wish to
 re-rehearse this shuttling.

All this disburdening light hurts your eyes. The woman in the next room
at the Hotel Parthenon sighs, a handkerchief of light over her navel

like the fine mesh catching snipes winding through the spaces between
 trees
toward an estuary resembling forgetfulness. In time, we'll try to parse the
 snipes too,

the clouds, the rotted trees.... We parse even the red epaulet on the shoulder
of the blackbird perched against the marshlands stretching into
 equatorial heat

where the buildings are certainly less monumental, sincere & aboriginal.
Maybe that's why tropical birds are larger with more elaborate plumage

than that of North American birds—one never knows what is considered
 beautiful,
even a tired woman in flats leaning against the snout of a stone lion

before a windowless government building, even the W.C. next to
>   Napoleon's tomb
where one places one's shoes in the embossed footprints of the floor

to relieve oneself, feeling as some monkeys must have felt when the jungle
burned to savannah, each one alone, ready to run full-tilt toward any light.

Natural History

Nurse sharks sleep a foot from the bottom,
or seem to, sand-colored stealth bombers.

I haven't been close enough to confirm this,
but Darwin assures me the food chain fathoms that deep.

I believe the Fish is right, Stanley Fish, that is—
each assertion displaces some other reticent fellow's

unpowerful sentence, a large grouper swallowed whole
below the coral reef off the coast of Florida.

No wonder the Buddhist masters brook not a word,
pointing at the moon. Imperative clarity.

The raven broadcasts its winter surplus with a shrill caw.
So there! On good days, not one monk goes up in orange flames,

the monks are feasting, the monkeys are fasting,
not a word, not a wind.

Acts of Privacy

A wind of red clover riffles each flame without blowing any out,

the water not blinking its bright eye, not once,
as the heron lifts its ash-blue wings to put distance between you...

the ten thousand things are one horse,
you have no reason to challenge Chuang Tzu:

the "this" and the "that" give birth to each other.
Nothing is complete or impaired.

Take, for instance, the roofless ceramics factory, 3 a.m.—
you're not there—two friends stare at the lunatic face of the moon,

a bottle of Chianti on a wicker strap between them,
rain suspended from the rotted boards like chandeliers.

On a cement slab, a half-finished head of Nefertiti

among broken shards of glazed Jesuses and glazed cats—
you skirt with these the last shadows of your dreamless sleep,

the abundance that has come to you in error,
the abundance that has come to you.

A Self-Portrait with Lucian Freud and Max Beckmann

In my book, time never ends, and the ultimate doesn't want to be
    worshipped.
Get off your knees. The hollyhocks turn imperceptibly toward the light
that comes through the mimosa's pink whiskers
the way plankton sift through the whale's microscopically fine cilia.

Why do I want the secret cut out? And cut out again?
Is the ache addictive? Can a ceiling fan turning the air in one room
flicker the light in the next? The true haunting is the unghostly room itself.

I'll never be purged of this childhood I remember so little of—
it is slivers of glass, waves continuously climbing back to the shore.
My mother's palm stung across my cheek is a petrogylph.
I knew I'd grow so different from her I'd have to bury her.

Identity is a bauble crushed in the fist.
That's why so much of life is janitorial, washing the windows,
moving the furniture from wall to wall as in a competition:
one of me is a small yellow bird.

One of me sits next to his reflection in a train window.
One of me sits on a porch, sipping a drink, counting off pills.

What if these avaricious appetites increase earth's bounty?
In one self-portrait, Lucian Freud is staring down from himself,
a ceiling lamp at the temple, forcing the viewer's eye back
so that seeing is a sinkhole swallowing an orchard
or a thunderhead cozying its jagged skein of light.

Death is a single face, this I've said elsewhere—you can check—
a single face no matter how facial muscles twist.
Max Beckmann's circus is, surprisingly, a comfort,
all the perverse masks summarized in the trapeze artist's wooden face
foregrounded so high up, the grin seems genuine....

I may be remembering this wrong, the way I need it.
The animal faces of man.
The way that jazz allows a riff to go off and play back against the others, so that the troubled whole somehow sounds right, if not to the ear, then to the brain which is continually firing out beyond its limits.

THREE

Against endings...

Song Not for the Orchid but for Knott

Way in the back of a makeshift nursery is an orchid.
Oh, do not ask what kind, suffice it to say: it's alive.
Its yellow-orange sepals and scent are reminiscent
of some ancient scenario you almost cannot recall.

Your pulse doesn't race anymore, unless the telephone,
its ring, actually, jolts you into morning, filling you with
the minor dreads and chores no one really need perform.
Day is like that, not like that sail-billow it takes to blow

the refrain Nat blasts on the cornet to signal "Arriving Soon."
Memory weans the dreamer from what was seen, sail
rising over a pale blue sea, white spume spun in curls,
all that crashing absolved of motives and ramifications

the way the bighorn sheep seem to pitch themselves off
when all they can avoid is crossing paths with the you
coming down the trail the other way, the clatter of hooves
barely carrying back from some surer footing not here.

The present is better off without much past, which shifts
automatically upon your looking back, rescoring it with
music trying to keep up with the late allegiance to a wave,
a quickening rubato above the time as if a rope were cut.

(NOTE: Nat Adderley plays cornet on Eddie Vinson's "Arriving Soon"
on The Cannonball Adderley Quintet Plus, Riverside, 1961, and his own
Talkin' About You, 32 Jazz, 1998.)

Miles from the Sea (Alternate Take)
for Curtis Fuller, trombone on "Undecided"

Out walking, you see a bottle of Cool Fish wine lying on the ground
at such an angle the sunlight passes through it, fish thrashing tails
across the curve so they look as if they're flying. This is preferred
to any still life, a cutting board of cod with their heads chopped.

Why do you believe there's something to this augury, tea leaves
twined in a cup of orange pekoe, crystals reenergized in seltzer,
an owl at the milk center of a fig bush? The future wants nothing,
sure the family long ago washed its hands of you, and therefore
you don't exist in any universe that time has to bother with.

Fuller's trombone vibrates like sea surf, even here, miles from the sea.
Since time never finishes, you could lie here till cataracts cross your eyes
and whisper that heaven is not a barracks, that heaven is not arrest,
and whisper your identification number like rain, like wind, like rain.

You're a petty criminal in a province in which everything is criminal.
Digging in the sand by an imaginary sea is punishable by ridicule.
They tie you to a post till rain begins to fall oily on your skin.
If you help them bind your limbs, of what are you culpable?
After a while, your skin turns bluish-yellow from the pollutants
suspended in the air that certain brave men have deemed fit to breathe.

Since time is risk, openness breathes your heart valves wide, and joy
ricochets its hummingbird's ruby-throated kindnesses, beak
stippling your temples where the sideburns are razor-trimmed.
The aqueducts begin a sloppy blues march. You're not dreaming.
This is an eventuality for which your circuitous ventures have primed you
like a fuel pump, readiness and all, everything and the kitchen sink,
as they should want to say, as is the way music happens when it happens
when you're not out cold, your body dogged-eared like a paperback.

Not for the Birds Blues

If what moves us along is the twisted logic of birds
as the wire door swings open without words, a click
against the cage proper, the cuttlebone already lonely,
and not one etched finch has flown, one long second
before openness is warped by flight and cross-flight,
one fear engendering a second, a third, and a fourth...
till all negotiation feels like the twisted loops of wire
shed from newspapers, part of one sliding underfoot
like a tap dancer's tap, the loop of another cuffing you
around the instep, then not, not even there, it may be
all right for me to think of the saxophonist Ben Webster
the day he died, all the wind gone out of his sax, legato,
its valves relaxed, unchurlish, girlish, bunched up with
the bedclothes and the hospital chart. And I'm thinking
what good would this do the anyone who thinks of it?
I won't think this: I won't hear the sweet gruff sounds
that sax Ol' Betsy might have blossomed if he lived on.
I won't think this. He has blown enough, sweet Ben,
on the late train to Naples, head lolling with sleep.

And I won't think about the affinities between my face
and the face of the man long dead. And I won't think
about Hawk and Bird. Not much anyway. Thinking
about suffering isn't literal suffering, even in a hovel
of a church off Beale where the ladies in nurses' uniforms
revive an overweight woman, rocking her head on her neck.
This joy is not an easy exultation, their bodies swaying
as if it were easier to bear the load of standing that way,
and it probably is, I can't say. I can say that, back then,
my knees wobbled the pews. My folks didn't sing, not
like Ben's, no, we kept the singing in till it negotiated
several forms of mental illness, a tree in the brain swaying
at the stem, slapping either hemisphere of the skull till
we assumed this throttling was par for the world's course,
famine folk refusing second best, desperate for heaven.

My Aunt Shirley used to argue with the woman next door
that the bush that divided their properties was lantana
while this woman, an Italian, swore it was pomegranate
but, without the hairy red seed-hoards, she seemed cracked,
though the flowers on this bush were a reddish orange
that always made me think of a red juice running a cheek,
and surely that's a subject for living dreams, so maybe
this woman has a point, since when I picked a blossom
and left it on the sill, the reddish hue darkened as it shriveled
to half its original size in an eyecup—the floral argument, too.

I don't need Ben's baleful "Lover, Come Back to Me."
My love is timely, always late with the sun long ensconced
in the big river west of here. I play the tune, play it loud
as a sort of paranoid's insurance, a birdsong mantra
now that July is running out and the purple martins'
morning song is an eerie absence lolling its head on the fence
for, around this time each year, migration begins again, fledglings
pretty much the same size as the adults, the iridescent males,
the pale-bellied females, each and every one gone, flying south,
some say as far as Belize, others, farther, as far as
the northern rain forests of Brazil. The birds must speak a host
of different languages, Spanish and Portuguese, at least,
as well as the hospitable united Southern drawl.
So, I'll have to depend on the recorded archives of exotic birds,
on record labels from Italy, the Netherlands and Denmark
where jazz is the enduring pleasure of surprise,
cats roaming unfixed the ancient monuments,
strong odors of every kind singing their nasty songs.
I wait for the weather to offer its correspondences.
I wait for the ants to launch toward that broken orange
oozing its juices in the street. Animals are compassionate,
take the raven in winter, the bees stippling the greenweed.
Man is a quick study, isn't he? Can't I depend on him and
the years coming on with mixed intentions? This isn't my first
and surely not my last. I'll be waiting. Lover, come back to me.

Our Mutant Gazes

Can you say it's a serious cartoon effect that you're after,
can you say that? That all the electrical appliances
with their plugs & outlets are hyper-aware of their femaleness &
   maleness?
That they are together right now at this moment with the juices flowing?

Can you say *that* is why, out of a sense of sexual accommodation,
you are walking by the sea,

which is not flowing in a sense so much as it's mistakenly in place
there upon the rocks, upon the homely rocks?

You can say that surely, you can say the gulls are holding a committee
   meeting,
and it is hard to perceive which one at this very moment is making a
   jackass of himself

because sooner than later they pitch their breasts into the wind
and flap their wings until the wind returns them
to a spot further off down the beach where, for them, you aren't.
Their moving off to be half a flock, an eighth of one, is communal, isn't it,

how accommodation requires the absenting of oneself for a while
from what might become essential

or the sustenance for the essential, which always occurs across a distance?

Why else would vistas surrender themselves to our mutant gazes,
to our mutilating gazes, how the past is always there in slivers
shooting back at us as if the shine of glass never penetrates the skin?

There is no skin upon these homely rocks unless the sea is a kind of skin.

The sand pounded upon itself sparkles like thousands of broken wine glasses.
You toss a mottled stone into the sea, a quiet craving, to cross
from language into the quiet most everyone else isn't interested in.

You watch the wheelchair athletes circle their infirmities above the bluff
beneath the haggard pathetic palms, spilling bottles of water over their heads

in order not to say a word-needing-a-return-word, just to breathe secretly as a flock.

You can be certain such wild acts inspire the actual wading birds, the ones
with the blunt, black, crimped beaks; they are nesting on the slope of rocks
off to the right, the slope bathed in sun, each nest off by itself, bathing.

Against Endings: Two Studies

What about one of Michelangelo's last Pietàs
in the maze of outbuildings at Sforza Castle, the dead Christ
visually carrying his mother
as she grows from his shoulder, a delicate marionette.
Like a sunflower along a road, her ginger face opens wizenly
as if she couldn't stand more looking.

How can stone shoulder such scant curiosity, the flesh unpolished
compared to the other, more famous examples of suffering?
Not this one—the sculptor himself cut short of time—
the bronze flesh vibrating as if emitting a nuclear wind.

What's more, the Christ has an extra, oversized arm, a tree to outgrow time,
a trunk for the dead to lean on upon a road to elsewhere
more or less on time, a leisure the great can lend themselves.

When a landscape is a portrait, there's hair growing on it
and arrows designating angles of perspective
which will remain undiscoverable, each eye a jag of lightning
wrapped in a sootbag as if lofted by some invisible giant tramp,
hobo, bum…there's so many stereotypes for what this stereotype doesn't do.
All we see is soot shimmering over a hill that looks like someone's shoulder.
It moves out to what is traditionally called a horizon, one of as many as hair.

In Gorky's memoirs, these men traveled in groups, sat in trees,
discussing the big ideas of the day. And the days went by
as did the implacable trains by night, blue hell on wheels
through the veins of sleeping boys and the veinless crucifixions

of rickety scarecrows shedding their rags to the wind
like formalities, even effigy crumbling to powder
unconfined by time and place so that the crows are unmistakably
black arrows circling themselves down to a tonsured spot
on the earth's pate. And there is no end to death's mercy.

In Memory of Bill Matthews

I must tell you what you know: the earth's not your element.
Faithless as ever, your knees crack in the official flames.

We mix you with sticks & manure to bonemeal the holes
that two young pear trees with their root-bags will overflow.

Welcoming you amid the orchard of the dead, multi-reed man
Eric Dolphy vaporizes the silence inside his flute to a dog's whistle.

Clifford Brown, Mingus, Young, Powell. Grief feeds its own.
In the seasons after you, white blossoms blowing a strange calm,

we'll come to admit that we can't end anything right,
killing a cabernet whose legs you'd skip across the sky for.

Your body not even a scent among the heifers in the scrub,
nightmare's carousel slows to the billow & collapse of breath,

twilight blowing on a point of wire, no cowbell
to begin the steady, slow nose-to-tail, no pastoral.

A Meditation Departing from Francis Bacon's
Oedipus and the Sphinx after Ingres, 1983

      1.

In jogging sweats, a man lifts his foot up on a step.
A wobbly gray circle pierces the muscles in his wrist
so he holds the pose, thinking he sees his face
in some winged bust—not in the cobbler's deserted glass
but reflected onto it from across the street.

Will there be a thousand other transparencies
thrown lightly against a wall?
When he turns, the face behind him is gone.
Is this face some future trying to forgive itself?

Things go a little farther away than he can reach,
the way ghosts turn through their pale linings and disappear.
Maybe that's what is meant by the word "preoccupied,"
that gaze that seems to have no object
but may have too many so that none, individually,
is the object of desire, though many linger
in their discretions: one die of a pair worn smooth by hands,
a woman's bone earring, someone's rotting knees.

Interior of a dream: the furniture is sparse, spare as it is in dream,
as it is in a lodging when money's scarce, temporary.

His father is lying on his side—on one palm,
a head round and addled as a head of lettuce.
The dead father is looking across the space
as if there were something to watch.
Out the window, a smokestack obscures the sky.

A faint voice says: this is somewhere foreign
where filth burgeons like flowers, gaudy flowers.

With his palm, the father brushes his hair back,
and the hair grows as fast as snakes shooting up a creek.
A man and his father listen to Ornette Coleman's petulant sax
as it lays a line down for Charlie Hayden's accents.
This oracle doubts itself, feels the damp accretions
on the cave walls and, from this strength, comes a voice
that makes a sound think newly about itself, even if it's ancient.

2.

I am jogging in purple sweat pants and my laces are flying—
a fast car's fender nearly under me. The driver does her best
to resist my irrepressible desire to be that kiss. She's trying even
as she wheels her car across a slight dip and into a pile of gravel.
I forgot to tell you, Dad, that on the bottom of the shoe
are a few lines from a poem I've been trying:

> *Bits of ash blow burnt on the wind, then stick to the water,*
> *which is dull and green and isn't the name for this.*
> *The deer's eyes are pellets of gray rice.*
>
> *The man steers across the sound, a blue motorized boat.*
> *Can the deer trust a man who blows like ash over water?*
>
> *The man cradles the deer's neck, the boat trembles, motorized.*
> *He backs off when it begins kicking, when blindness begins kicking*
> *as if, lopped off by the mind, the moment isolates. We know*
> *the tide ripple never finishes. There are no proper names for this.*
> *Isn't intimacy uninhabited if a man is truly in it?*

That's as far as I've got. What do you think? Your silence
spurs me now as much as it ever did. The man is neither one of us,
not that close: he tips the deer as he clutches it—to shift the ache.
The poem is missing something, but what, exactly, I can't say,

the way I can't say if it's right to spill the oil on the catfish,
the coconut milk, the galanga root finely minced, pulverized lemon grass,
salt, peppercorns crushed with just the right amount of tomato sauce.
Actually, I eyeball it till the roux's the saffron color of Buddhist robes.
Maybe the other deer wade into the water on the far side of the island,
keeping their black mouths up to breathe. Some charities are just beyond
our capacities. Our capacities are easier than we say.

I kick the last leg home: the redwing blackbirds oilcan the pines.
Below: a three-legged typing table, some perforated, rain-warped pegboard
above an economy box of Cheer with its tongue ripped out.

Language
for Paul Naylor

Boy toy, bell buoy: "didn't I tell you this thing wouldn't work?"
the recalcitrance of words nothing new
the way we called the large dark-brown nuts what our parents taught us—
Nigger Toes—out of a larger ignorance than God or Physics,
the ballooning largess of the apple tree blossoms
along Decatur inviting us to
the divvying up of the rain
like applause, applause like rain.

Along U.S. 82 East, the light off the greenhouses
is like the spume Hart Crane barely teetered above—
an emerald or tourmaline with tints of fire—
before he leapt into the sea,
the salt words choking him,
his eye an anise clove sweetening all it soon couldn't see.

Fee-Fi-Fo-Fum (Alternate Take)

Like the opacity of gym glass, their stories of innocence and punishment,
the easy eradication of the crows. These men soap their chests white,
then glide quiet and virulent through the changing room, with towels.

Only the tattoos distinguish them. They tell how they discharge shotguns
in the elms and the maples, and how the murder disappears,
all wings, into another tree. Long ago, I stared right into the sun

during an eclipse because they had said not to do so, the blowhards,
the hot air making the clouds and sea seem all one thing,
some black ice bound to thrash us on our spines, coccyges cracked,

sliding out on the void our breath creates. *C'est la vie, c'est la guerre,*
and people clinging to these catch-alls the way grime does to filters,
coffee grounds in a ditch of paper. *Here's the church, here's the steeple.*

No one ever woke up desperately in love with us, no one short of breath
to the point of asphyxiation, paramedics arriving with solemn manner,
their faces like those on the kids forced to attend a birthday, balloons

over tubs of harlequin ice cream, the strawberry melting in the heat.
We pay respect to our past selves, as if they were jars of beets
and some proud slacker had turned each top to hear the wheeze

of airtight freshness escape into what is now the neighborhood,
give or take the hundred ancillary noises, a car backfiring, the crickets
counting their pennies, a dog's cough. And, tonight, thanks to the heat,

we have our own set of luna moths affixed to the backdoor screen,
wanting in, wanting in, these separate identities.
I'm forgetting more as I grow older, maybe that's what aging is,

slipping like time into the future, gone as soon as it pipes up, *here, chief,*
having shown up for roll call. We grow calmer about effacement
as the days roll out their finest hours and the festivities dust flour off,

there, all clean. That's how it should be, the itch of a dream we can't
    scratch.
The more we obsess about vines bringing a chain-link to its knees the
    more
we pull and pull and then just give up, the thicket looking pretty much as it

has always looked, overgrown with mosquitoes, birds mum with tearing.
And what about the kids, off at the movies, sucking their collective breath
as the damp mezzanine closes in on inarticulate fears they feed more candy?

I blush about the excitement still partly in my blood from when Heston
as the Cid made his horse clop across the sand, the epic bag of goods
they'd sold us before we were old enough to know better, stupid strength,
not even a brain synapse, some kind day, to divest ourselves of this.

Yes I Can, No You Can't (Endless Takes)

The pristine slate of the moment is not comforting, and not true,
but who's to blame? You're the one doing the talking, the same shimmy
you've done for years, lisping bottom lines with sharpened pencils
while the accounting major in you would have done better to go fishing
at the crooked drink where catfish are said to still breed in the mud,
if such intricacy hasn't become anathema in the interim, while you were
    out,
one holier-than-thou revision of your first gut-honest response,

and who's to say which of the sacrifices on the menu is bound to save us,
collectively or not, when the calibrations are so limited, numb
from flying like moths, feet to the flame, and back, scorched
and keeping the vast hurt to ourselves, as we had been taught by ghosts
who couldn't feel their shadows and so passed nearly wholeheartedly into us:
their neurasthenic charges—crass maroon ties, pressed white shirts?

One Sister of St. Joseph bragged about a crack in the blackboard,
the threatened O'Connell head proving time an illusion, our classmate
three years his brother's junior—and the crack's—the nun rising
from her crucible, a night lamp for soldiers who cast lots for Jesus's robes,
a blood rope seeping down her roughhewn rosary cinch and rood.

You can't wipe ignorance off your hands—it collects in the seams
along with the yellow chalk dust gathered in the erasers. Yellow plumes!
What sadists would make kids clap these things out behind the school
where the hoarse throats of milk cartons belch their sour breath, the iron
Dooley Dumpster a modern oracle for hiding cigarettes? Sweet censer smoke

    and punishment, early on, we sensed that God was more interesting than
        that.
    Or what we could unimagine of things as frightening as mercy and
        contemplation.
    What teeter-totters when time and place shift is what's holy, circumstances
        altered or continuously trembling. It seemed emblematic, the little fiction
            with legs,

the ants you saw in Kansas, an insect zoo, each carrying a pale green leaf,
its fragrant baggage, down a transparent pipe—in one wall and out
    another—
the mind's mansion from which at times you find yourself locked out,
    circling,
the cadence of your step a vamp to steady the notes you bend to the
    breaking point,
like the time you woke afraid to reclose your eyes because you had dreamt
    yourself
imminently dead, literally, rising to meet it as if on a serving tray, and
    whether it lifted you,
like finger food or not, depended on your eyes killing forever the efficacy
    of dreams.

Black Expatriate Playing near the Ligurian Sea

Calvin Massey: "*When are you coming back?*"
Don Byas: "*When they build a bridge!*"

Tatum convinces Byas there aren't any wrong notes
as long as he keeps playing,
like a Manx tumbling from a window box of red flowers,
the cat already somewhere else, licking a bubble of cream.

You're not looking close enough to see the flowers move,
a brown knuckle creasing an ivory. The red pigment, too,
off somewhere, the venture's a matter of breathing, a sequence
you aren't permitted to trigger—your point of view the alien thing

introduced to openness as the train brakes beside a platform,
the moist night air like an arpeggio rushing you along,
a brutality that hasn't surrendered its beauty.
Byas plays "Six, Seven, Eight, or Nine," the sax like ice
writing its invite to the vehemence of the All-Unaquiring
like that climbing vine that grows for years without blossoms
saved for a later, different you, happiness having nothing to do with it,
moving between shipyard and the mottled cliff shoring up lives
you can't ever story enough, the letters of your name rising on thermals.

Everything breathes and transpires, that's what you work back to,
a world given without givens, the act of never innocent, never
guilty either, something that changes whether you look away
or join it, the gesture's motioning the quality of acquiescence—
the sparks a blowtorch scatters over the gray hull of a ship.

Atonal Raindrops in the Flyway, After Cecil Taylor

The rain hits each leaf separately, the fig tree's, the mimosa's,
and the leaves still a few drops,
the sun reflected on each like a close-up lens
on a silver-backed beetle, a fisheye of witch hazel.

The mimosa's pink oversize eyelash
is a drag queen's impeccable sympathy,
certainly "peck-able," given this is the flyway
for three hundred and three species,
give or take the attrition of adolescent birds
blown off track by winds and powerlines.

Of course such particularity demands something we can agree on
as central to the silences facing off around this thing
we haven't as yet chosen,
while people everywhere testify to the limits
of its centrifugal force, the way centering a room around a trophy—
All-City, All-Conference, All-Catholic—
debilitates what one thinks about oneself after a while,
after the gilt peels or the statuette's screw loosens
and the picture window, day after day,
highjacks the room out to its illumination of endless vines.

Then the drops re-drop with a wind through the bigger, taller trees,
scattering thoughts that dampen the inside of a collar
—the icicle instant—and the next few seconds
seem a respite from falling things. But the sky offers none,
not even the net of clouds that seem, for the most part, innocuous,
or, at least, incidental, causing the mind to shimmy between itself
and a nondescript nether thing, worry stone or talisman.

Watch it! One straight from the open sky tilts your glasses.
The future turns its back, the moment you lose
in stopping to contemplate it, the irascible shirt tail
smearing the blotted lens. Another cold plop
third-eyeballs you as you step off the curb, embarrassed, anointed.
You're back in the cemetery among those who tied you to a tree.
It's a cold day in 1956 or 1957, it ruptures in dreams.
One of them lets you taste the salt on the back of his hand,
swears you to a secret that rain obliterates. The names cut in stone,
even those that stuffed your tongue above all that spit, are gone
like spindrift as soon as the sun's up and hunting the ground.
All you can taste is the humiliation wetting your extremities,
the way Saint Sebastian must have felt,
his strength sapped by arrows, the quick meeting the quick.

Attar of Violet & Loneliness

Things are growing, but not collective yet.
    A shadow bank has shifted like a dirigible

dropping water balloons of moisture, small collected lakes.
    When the sun returns,

thoughts will trellis whatever can gather itself up into the air.
    Then the day will reconsider things

the way a riding mower floats above swaths of earth
    so that the world, for a while,

seems an extension of our effort, a product of what we say.
    Drop cloths will float down over roses

and gutters will channel the downpours
    into some reservoir of waiting insatiable gravel,

some inland heavenly groundwater, attar of violet.
    And this is where it will have to stay,

this grievous joy, away from us who give it away
    with every little whispering mouth.

A Series of Photos for the Adoption Agency

Your glasses are strafed with sun.
The gravel above where your shoulders touch
detracts from the curve of your wife's neck.
There can be no space at all between you.

The human is not arboreal, the branch
mistakenly growing from your ear to the top of her head.
The crease inside your right eye down and along the bottom of the cheek
opens the sinus cavity of embarrassed breath.

Now here's a pair of helium heads floating the top of the fence,
the ruddy-cheeked fruit unevolved from the shoulders,
even as hills a bit too much for the neurasthenic child
who won't even see the photo till too late, if, by then,
the alien has rendered itself atavistic. But even these vulnerabilities

won't help the birth mother give away the face that resembles hers,
that takes her lover's with it so she can die somehow on the spot,
accept beauty, loss, the way the retina, detached at the back of the eye,
lets human folly wholly composed pass through the impervious,
lips pressed tight to hide the shade of each tooth, hair slicked back
on the cream-tiled mosque of the forehead, greed hidden by grief
and propelling it through what smoothes the features into place.

What if her Raphaelite hair is a low adumbration of fire,
a nervousness, her eyes shimmering Mexican agates?
Is it possible to feel each garish fear as it slogs deeper in the earth?
You feel the quickening of each newborn breath,
each blue canary's song lifted for the first time into the air.

Each branch, each leaf vein, axil and bole is a family tree,
a tree of the family—those taken up with those abandoned outright,
the abscesses and arabesques of absentees who won't die
in the male and female of a single face, who won't die in the angle of time

with desire's face. No one wishes the whole world wholly back, sources of light leaking from fields where the originating act continues in the walleyed divergence of portrait and profile, a crouching figure in the grass suddenly wet with day.

The Blind Man, Twilight Turning Night

    Is it cardinals

that separate seed from the yellow blades of rye
the way braille comes up with the fingertips,

    those russet *chips*

and silences, scarlet, sharp as flax…?
Soon, next door, the college kids tip their glasses

    to the falling stars.

In here, where I see, they're all stars, a slow motion
of blood & bone, a quick harem of browns

    then one scarlet slur

curving the sky, my arm between the hand & shoulder
like a magician's long string of silk handkerchiefs

    blown from the dark.

These Continuous Things

So whether or not I'm remembering as the constant wind remembers,
the bridge begins swaying slowly at first,
then violently till it looks like a helix just as it breaks apart

splashing into the strong current. But to say so with verbs shunting nouns
is probably as repulsive & insistent as gravity is
to the chunks of concrete threaded with steel cable, cracking, snapping.

In the past, you'd have insisted on the link between jubilation &
    punishment,
between expectation & imminence, but now the past is yeast inside the
    future
offering a premonition that is no longer trustworthy,

a clear rehearsal of what will not be really going on, as if it were.
Why is it that, in older countries, illusion can brood on blood inseparable
    from time,
feel bad about itself & still show up wearing an ostentatious red hat at the
    party?

Oh hell, any hat is ostentatious, every one, so illusion can live its whole life
and there isn't necessarily a problem with the established landscape.
Here, there is a trestle through which you can see blue eyelets of water.

Here, the climbing vines luxuriate, suffocating everything too pale to bleed.
You pull one clear of any connection & let the wind have a long tress of hair.
You pull it clear like rehearsal, watching the drift with a precision that
    relents,

the sleeve of little flowers with hair-like petals effortlessly drifting down
among shadows you can barely see because the most obvious gestures are
    invisible
to the happy ones who say they love flags & what flags stand for,

the shiver of a flag's shadow, the clank of the pulley striking twice into
    silence—
the national worry doll of shadow in everyone's close pocket.
You are what the shadow worries, in the commonwealth, in the province,

in the hood, in the parish, the wheelhouse, the bailiwick, the....
You couldn't describe these continuous things...the roads, the half-moon.
Nothing is inside you. On the veranda of an antebellum mansion,

instead of throwing rice, the guests are blowing bubbles through plastic
    rings.
The river is exposing its sickly gums, but, just inside the foyer,
the pastel dresses are large lanterns rocking ritualistic happiness. The
    bride's father,

as ritual will have it, wears a moustache & is as thin as a knotted vine.
He giggles in a way that you want to know him for the rest of your
    miserable life
now that you think of it, the river another flag, another shadow, the Yazoo,
    think of it,

a river with a name like this, the shadow with a name like this, kids like
    these
pushing down it on a makeshift raft that looks like a stage wig on fire,
a cloud lit from beneath by a dying sun—two striated floating barrels.

Dream Riffs off Oktoc Road

Time isn't the enemy, it's not maneuvering battalions across a field,
nor holding cavalry in reserve somewhere off in the forest shadows.
Several delicate coronas open themselves at the right hand. At the left
is a bird turning russet as we lip-sync these words across parchment,

no, across modern stiff 20-weight paper. The bird pinches a flower—
call it rapture, its yellow center spoking white and then violet ends,
each a two-inch span multiplied by the hundreds, the way Bill Evans's
fingers triple the silence as Scott LaFaro's bass throbs the heart slower

than it was ever meant to beat. Sure it's good to lower the head to listen
to the belly of a kit fox unable to extricate itself from rusted fence wire.
The kit nips its Samaritan, drumstick flicked against the drum's metal rim.
Time isn't the enemy. Sun rounds a melon in the warm canto of the earth.

Any other time would be nifty, but you want the designated time, the one
you got in your head, comfy-like, like a triangular bookcase in a corner
set off so well it disappears there, raising its own bank of off-shore fog,
the particles trapped in hovering discernible droplets. This is your anthem,

this silence at the other end of the line. Then it's a counter-rhythm, some
instrumental anti-accompaniment, a quick shrill sound rounding into rage
that can't express itself, that must hide in the damp corridors of the veins.
By turns, the trumpet, then the saxophone, swoops high above a gravel pit,

the sighs laid out by ancillary brass crucial to the peal's height, almost as if
each might break the ensemble, the way voice escapes word, the way a bull—
having burst confinement—stops and starts, startled by what sounds errant
to its flapping ears, then stumbles, snorts, legs splayed, frustrated and tired.

After a while, the eager rhythm section corrals the almost stray trajectories
that begin to pretend they'll behave—pale yellow honeysuckle at the hinds,
as if for ancient nuptials. Twilight, the old barn begins traipsing its gait
across the shadow of rafters, the wind through the loft an eerie, lovely cry.

About the Author

RICHARD LYONS's collections include *These Modern Nights* and *Hours of the Cardinal*. A past winner of the Lavan Award from the Academy of American Poets and The Discovery Award from *The Nation*, Lyons teaches at Mississippi State University where he is the director of the creative writing emphasis.

Photo by Leah Giniusz

About the Artist

HAMLETT DOBBINS was born in Knoxville, Tennessee. He received his B.F.A. from the University of Memphis and received his M.A. and M.F.A. from the University of Iowa. He is a recipient of the Pollock-Krasner Grant and the Tennessee Arts Commission Individual Artist Fellowship. His work has been featured in group and solo shows in Memphis, Chicago, New York, and Amsterdam. When he is not painting, he works as the director of Clough-Hanson Gallery at Rhodes College in Memphis where he lives with his wife and two children.

About the Washington Prize

Fleur Carnivore is the winner of the 2005 WORD WORKS Washington Prize. Richard Lyons' manuscript was selected from among 340 manuscripts submitted by American poets.

FIRST READERS:
    Nancy Allinson
    Doris Brody
    Don Cunningham
    Mark Dawson
    Colin Flanigan
    Elizabeth Hazen
    Erich Hintze
    Tod Ibrahim
    Sydney March
    Mike McDermott
    Angelin Tubman
    Jill Tunick
    Doug Wilkinson
    Marcella Wolfe

SECOND READERS:
    Sandra Beasley
    Brandon D. Johnson
    Steven B. Rogers

FINAL JUDGES:
    Karren L. Alenier
    J.H. Beall
    Bernadette Geyer
    Miles David Moore
    Ann Rayburn

About the Word Works

The Word Works, a nonprofit literary organization, publishes contemporary poetry in collectors' editions. Since 1981, the organization has sponsored the Washington Prize, a $1,500 award to an American poet. Monthly, The Word Works presents free literary programs in the Chevy Chase Café Muse series, and each summer, free poetry programs are held at the historic Joaquin Miller Cabin in Washington, DC's Rock Creek Park. Annually, two high school students debut in the Miller Cabin Series as winners of the Young Poets Competition.

Since 1974, Word Works programs have included: "In the Shadow of the Capitol," a symposium and archival project on the African-American intellectual community in segregated Washington, DC; the Gunston Arts Center Poetry Series (Ai, Carolyn Forché, Stanley Kunitz, and others); the Poet-Editor panel discussions at the Bethesda Writer's Center (John Hollander, Maurice English, Anthony Hecht, Josephine Jacobsen, and others); Poet's Jam, a multi-arts program series featuring poetry in performance; a poetry workshop at the Center for Creative Non-Violence (CCNV) shelter; and the Arts Retreat in Tuscany. Master Class workshops, an ongoing program, have featured Agha Shahid Ali, Thomas Lux, and Marilyn Nelson.

In 2006, Word Works will have published 60 titles, including work from such authors as Deirdra Baldwin, J.H. Beall, Christopher Bursk, John Pauker, Edward Weismiller, and Mac Wellman. Currently, The Word Works publishes books and occasional anthologies under three imprints: the Washington Prize, the Capital Collection, and International Editions.

Past grants have been awarded by the National Endowment for the Arts, National Endowment for the Humanities, DC Commission on the Arts & Humanities, Witter Bynner Foundation, Writer's Center, Bell Atlantic, Batir Foundation, and others, including many generous private patrons.

The Word Works has established an archive of artistic and administrative materials in the Washington Writing Archive housed in the George Washington University Gelman Library.

Please enclose a self-addressed, stamped envelope with all inquiries.

The Word Works   PO Box 42164   Washington, DC 20015
editor@wordworksdc.com   www.wordworksdc.com

Word Works Books

Karren L. Alenier, *Wandering on the Outside*
Karren L. Alenier, Hilary Tham, Miles David Moore, eds.,
   Winners: A Retrospective of the Washington Prize
* Nathalie F. Anderson, *Following Fred Astaire*
* Michael Atkinson, *One Hundred Children Waiting for a Train*
Mel Belin, *Flesh That Was Chrysalis* (CAPITAL COLLECTION)
* Carrie Bennett, *biography of water*
* Peter Blair, *Last Heat*
Doris Brody, *Judging the Distance* (CAPITAL COLLECTION)
Grace Cavalieri, *Pinecrest Rest Haven* (CAPITAL COLLECTION)
Christopher Conlon, *Gilbert and Garbo in Love*
   (CAPITAL COLLECTION)
Donna Denizé, *Broken Like Job* (CAPITAL COLLECTION)
Moshe Dor, Barbara Goldberg, Giora Leshem, eds.,
   The Stones Remember
* Linda Lee Harper, *Toward Desire*
James Hopkins, *Eight Pale Women* (CAPITAL COLLECTION)
* Ann Rae Jonas, *A Diamond Is Hard But Not Tough*
Myong-Hee Kim, *Crow's Eye View: The Infamy of Lee Sang,*
   Korean Poet (INTERNATIONAL EDITIONS)
Vladimir Levchev, *Black Book of the Endangered Species*
   (INTERNATIONAL EDITIONS)
* Fred Marchant, *Tipping Point*
Judith McCombs, *The Habit of Fire* (CAPITAL COLLECTION)
* Ron Mohring, *Survivable World*
Miles David Moore, *The Bears of Paris* (CAPITAL COLLECTION)
Miles David Moore, *Rollercoaster* (CAPITAL COLLECTION)
Jacklyn Potter, Dwaine Rieves, Gary Stein, eds.
   Cabin Fever: Poets at Joaquin Miller's Cabin
* Jay Rogoff, *The Cutoff*
Robert Sargent, *Aspects of a Southern Story*
Robert Sargent, *A Woman From Memphis*
* Enid Shomer, *Stalking the Florida Panther*
Maria Terrone, *The Bodies We Were Loaned* (CAPITAL COLLECTION)
Hilary Tham, *Bad Names for Women* (CAPITAL COLLECTION)
Hilary Tham, *Counting* (CAPITAL COLLECTION)
Jonathan Vaile, *Blue Cowboy* (CAPITAL COLLECTION)
* Miles Waggener, *Phoenix Suites*
* George Young, *Spinoza's Mouse*

   * Washington Prize winners

Travels on the Road Not Taken

Towards a Bible-Based Theory of Jewish Spirituality

Travels on the Road Not Taken

Towards a Bible-Based Theory of Jewish Spirituality

Martin Samuel Cohen

Copyright © 1997 Martin Samuel Cohen

No part of this publication may be reproduced, stored in a retrieval system or transmitted in any form or by any means without the prior written permission of the publisher.

Cover Art by Karon E. Mitton
Cover Collage by the author, based on 1 Chronicles 25:4
Cover Design by Pinpoint Publications Limited
Printed and bound in Canada

Canadian Cataloguing in Publication Data

Cohen, Martin Samuel, 1953-
  Travels on the road not taken : towards a Bible-based theory of Jewish Spirituality

ISBN 0-920259-62-6

1. Bible. O.T. Psalms - Criticism, interpretation, etc., Jewish.
2. Spirituality - Judaism. I. Title.

BS1430.2.C63 1997   223'.206   C97-931015-6

Moonstone Press
167 Delaware Street
London, Ontario
Canada N5Z 2N6

The lamp of God had not yet gone out,
but Samuel was already asleep in the temple of the Lord ...
    The Book of Samuel

All genuine knowledge originates in direct experience.
    Mao Zedong

The fear of God leads to the study of Scripture.
    Sifri Deuteronomy

... The Organist is hee
Who hath tun'd God and Man, the Organ we.
The songs are these, which heavens high holy Muse
Whisper'd to David, David to the Jewes.
And Davids Successors, in holy zeale,
In formes of joy and art doe re-reveale ....
    John Donne

One thing have I asked of the Lord, one thing shall I seek:
to live in the house of the Lord all the days of my life, to gaze upon the
beauty of the Lord, to tarry in His Temple (Psalm 27:4).
Rabbi Elimelech asked, "Are living, seeing
and tarrying then the same one thing?"
Rabbi Elimelech answered his own question:
"If the object of an individual's yearning is one,
then how can the truth be otherwise?"
    Elimelech Weissbrot

I arise at midnight ....
    The Psalms

Contents

Author's Note 9
Preface 11
1. What's In It For Me? 15
2. What the Chronicler Thought 24
3. A Different Man 30
4. Seeing God 35
5. And Hearing His Voice 40
6. What We Could Have Been 43
7. Asleep in the Temple 48
8. *Kên Baqqodesh Ḥazitikhah* 55
9. *'Esbeʻah Behaqitz Temunatekhah* 64
10. *'Aḥat Sha'alti* 72
11. *Yêshvu Yesharim 'Et Panekhah* 77
12. *Yoshêv Hakkeruvim Hofiʻah* 83
13. *Mitziyyon 'Elohim Hofiʻa* 88
14. *ʻAnêni* 93
15. *Zeh Hashaʻar* 98
16. *Sefat Loʼ Yadaʻti 'Eshmaʻ* 101
Epilogue: *Lo Navi 'Anokhi* 106
Bibliographical Notes 117
About the Author 142

Author's Note

There are any number of important Jewish commentators on the Bible who are known to their readers by acronyms formed of the initial letters of the various parts of their names or by patronymics. In the following work, Rashi stands for *R*abbi *Sh*lomo *Y*itzchaki of Troyes (1040-1105), generally acclaimed as the most authoritative Jewish commentator on the Bible in the medieval period. Ibn Ezra is Abraham Ibn Ezra (1080-1164), one of the two or three greatest Spanish Jewish commentators. Radak is *R*abbi *D*avid *K*imchi of Narbonne (1157-1236), one of the most prominent Provençal rabbis and authors. Ramban is *R*abbi *M*oses *b*en *N*achman (1194-1270), also called Nachmanides, another one of the most important Spanish commentators on Bible and Talmud and a major kabbalist in his own right. The Meiri is Rabbi Menachem bar Shlomo Meiri (1249-1316) of France. Sforno is Ovadiah ben Yaakov Sforno (1475-1550), an Italian scholar and physician. The Rid is *R*abbi *I*saiah ben *D*avid of Trani (c. 1200-c. 1260), a well known Italian scholar and a particularly insightful commentator on the Books of Samuel.

Liberal use has been made of the translation of the Bible published over many years and completed in 1985 by the Jewish Publication Society in Philadelphia. I have, however, departed from their translation at will and many passages appear in my own translation from the start. Passages that appear in others' translations are all indicated clearly in the notes to each chapter.

In this book, I have used the letter h with a dot beneath it to represent the Hebrew letter *ḥet*. *Ḥet* has roughly the same sound as the *ch* at the end of Ba*ch*. Proper names are mostly presented in their familiar form, however.

I've also used masculine pronouns to refer to the authors of the various psalms despite the fact that I have no idea whether they were men or women. This was a stylistic decision based on the desire to avoid having to write "he or she" or "his or her" over and over. Given the fact that the author of the Book of Chronicles was probably thinking of the reality he knew in his own day when he specifically noted that both men and women served as Levitical singers in the First Temple, one could argue that this usage is as historically misleading as it is, to use the loathsome phrase, politically incorrect. Still, wherever the Hebrew does betray the gender of an author within the Psalter, the indication is that the author was male and so we can feel certain that at least some, probably most and possibly - if only possibly - all of the poets whose works are included among the psalms were men. My decision was to opt for grace of style rather than either strict historical accuracy or gender neutrality and, for better or worse, I acknowledge here the arbitrariness of that decision.

A certain portion of the epilogue appeared in the summer of 1996 as part of an article published in the journal *Conservative Judaism*. Some paragraphs that appear in the first six chapters of this book are taken from an essay on the spirituality of the Psalms scheduled for publication in that journal later this year.

The terms *pre-exilic*, *exilic* and *post-exilic* used throughout this book refer to the half century of exile in Babylon endured by the leading citizens of the ancient kingdom of Judah in the sixth century B.C.E. Widely acknowledged as the pivotal experience in the historical experience of ancient Israel, the exile prompted the production of almost all the books of the Hebrew Bible and, for that reason alone, must be seen as one of the truly definitive events of Israelite antiquity. The exile in Babylon was, at any rate, the catalyst that, for better or worse, effected the transformation of the religion of the ancient Israelites into the earliest form of Judaism.

Finally, the sources for all quotes and Biblical allusions mentioned in this book are listed chapter by chapter immediately following the epilogue.

M.S.C.
May 18, 1997
Richmond, B.C.

Preface

There are always two ways.

The way of Judaism is the way of Torah as set down in the five-part book we call *the* Torah. It is the way of law and commandment, of service and ceremony, of fealty and obedience. It is the spiritual path of earthly souls who feel themselves bidden to serve the God of Heaven in roughly the same way faithful and obedient servants in any manor house serve their lords and masters: with zeal, with humility and with submissive, unquestioning loyalty. It is the way of the ancient priesthood developed in countless ways over two dozen centuries into a religion of moderns.

Indeed, modern scholars have almost universally concluded that *the* Torah is *a* priestly work composed of mostly priestly material stretched over a literary frame designed to highlight the theological issues, spiritual stances and ritual postures that grew out of the priestly experience in ancient Israel. More than anyone else, these priests, specifically the Temple priesthood of old Jerusalem, were responsible for transforming the faith of their Israelite ancestors into the religion of Judah. That even today our Judaism is essentially their Judah-ism is testimony both to the power of their vision and to the enduring quality of their spiritual enterprise.

But there was also another way in antiquity, a way that offered its proponents a different kind of spiritual focus. It was a way of seeking God through direct experiential encounter, a method of spiritual enterprise rooted in the kind of faith that flows from sensual experience of the divine rather than the kind that develops from compliance to pre-determined rules and regulations. It too produced a five-part work that became a classic of spiritual literature, a book destined to live on as one of the greatest gifts of Israel to the world. This other book is the Psalter, the Book of Psalms, the book Jews call *Tehillim* or, more colloquially, *Tillim*. And the kind of religion it proposes to its readers is the religion of the prophet, the other pole of ancient Israelite faith.

That the priests and the prophets of ancient times didn't much care for each other is obvious from the books they left behind. The Torah itself barely mentions the prophets, failing (mostly) even to nod to them as it develops the almost incredibly complex set of rules and regulations that govern sacrifice and worship in the desert sanctuary intended to preshadow (and thus also, *ipso facto*, to validate as quintessentially authentic) the service of the priests in the Jerusalem temple. Indeed, the Torah's bias against the prophetic experience is glaring: not only are the prophets specifically *not* to be supported with anything resembling the elaborate system of taxation designed to support the priests, but the Torah hardly acknowledges the existence of the prophetic caste at all, turning to them basically only to warn Israel against prophetic apostates or false, self-appointed prophets who wilfully utter phoney oracles they themselves have made up ... or to note rather anachronistically that, in any event, the whole institution was degenerate in that none of the other prophets was ever to be Moses' equal anyway.

True, the Torah does promise that a prophet "like Moses" will appear someday to convey the true word of God to the people, but this development is assigned to the hazy future and seems quite pointedly to be referring to a single individual and specifically *not* to groups of people destined to function within society as an active, spiritual force - and the actual prophetic caste as it functioned in ancient Israel is left unacknowledged, thereby (at least for latter-day readers) delegitimized. Indeed, even the way the Torah uses the regular Hebrew word for prophet, *navi'*, is instructive. Used in the passages mentioned above to denote renegade and apostate prophets, it is also used in the Torah in an almost off-handed, rather dismissive way simply to mean "spokesman", almost as though to hint that the (other, mostly unacknowledged, unmentioned) prophets were merely the loudspeakers through which God chose to broadcast His word to the people from time to time rather than spiritual leaders of the people in their own right. (The fact that the passage to which I am referring specifically labels Aaron, the future High Priest himself, that way only makes the point more piquant. Another passage refers to Miriam, sister of Moses and Aaron, as a prophetess as well - despite the fact that one of the most famous stories about prophecy in the Torah specifically tells how God Himself specifically *didn't* appear to recognize either Miriam *or* Aaron as prophets when He discussed the nature of the prophetic experience with them both.) And nowhere at all is there any indication of a priestly concession to the fact that the prophets of Israel were promulgating a different kind of spiritual communion with God than the priests themselves were offering as *their* spiritual wares.

For its part, the Psalter is as uninterested in the priesthood as the Torah is in the prophetic caste - almost nowhere in the Book of Psalms do we find long (or even short) passages extolling *its* virtues or presenting the priest as the ideal role model for the aspiring Israelite worshipper. On the other hand, none of this means that the psalmists had no interest in Jerusalem or its great Temple other than in writing dismissively about its priests and disparagingly about the sacrificial worship service carried out within its sacred perimeters. Indeed, the poets invite their readers to step up and peep into the Temple's courts and forecourts in dozens of passages, but the scenes they offer the willing reader very specifically do not feature priests in the starring roles at all, but rather (mostly) unnamed others instead...others who gather at night in the sacred precincts to preserve and promulgate a kind of alternate spirituality, others who face the triple threats of calumny, verbal abuse and physical violence at the hands of brutal, unprincipled enemies on a daily basis, others who participate in strange, unfamiliar rituals designed to provoke mysterious encounters with the divine and who yearn to see the light of God's face, to hear God's voice and to experience the presence of God palpably, sensually and absolutely really...and who are depicted as having been at least occasionally successful in their efforts.

In a certain sense, this book is about those mysterious figures the poets saw lurking in the shadows of the darkened Temple, about who they were and what they did and how we, so many centuries later, can learn from them and build on their work. This is, therefore, not precisely a work of scholarship *or* one of theology, but rather a sort of hybrid intended to challenge as much as to inform.

I should probably conclude by stating openly that all of this constitutes a major step forward in my own thinking about the religion to which I have devoted my personal spirituality and professional career for all of my adult life. I know that some of what follows will strike any number of colleagues and friends as iconoclastic, but I also think that there are times when saying nothing is itself a kind of self-betrayal.

Many colleagues, students and friends have encouraged me to continue writing over the years and I would like to acknowledge their support in the hope that they all know who they are. To them, and to the directors and membership of the Beth Tikvah Congregation and Centre Association in Richmond, British Columbia, all of whom have encouraged my writing over these many years, my most sincere gratitude.

1. What's In It For Me?

There are always two ways.
The outer trappings of human civilization - the outfits people wear and the contraptions they use to get themselves around town and the procedures they devise to adjudicate disputes between otherwise friendly neighbours - these all change relentlessly, even inexorably, from generation to generation. We admire these developments and write books about them as though it were self-evident that these kinds of innovation are the undeniable signs of genuine growth - cultural advancements and societal improvements to be desired, fostered and ultimately (and deeply) cherished by those whose lives they transform.

But for all the outside shifts and alters, the basic aspects of human life remain, generation after generation, unchanging and unchanged. The yearning for meaning, for love, for health, for power over destiny, for obedient children, for happiness - these are constants that do not appear to vary at all from century to century. Just to the contrary, they collectively form the unyielding frame of earthly existence that suffers a bit of gilt or a wash of stain from time to time, but which otherwise remains intact and unaltered as a silent frame*work* across which the unfolding story of human history is stretched.

The questions people ask of their spiritual leaders appear to me to belong to the latter category. Where is God? How do I know there is a God? Is it possible to know what God wants of men and women below? What visible, empirically verifiable proof is there that the good we encounter in the course of our lives comes to us as a result of the blessing of God? And what proof is there that the specific rituals and rites that constitute the service we are taught to render unto God - what proof is there that that service has the same meaning to God that the terrestrials who devised it in the first place so fervently wished it to have?

Again and again, the Torah returns to the question of the rewards the pious may reasonably expect in exchange for their professions of faith and their efforts at worship. It may sound slightly ignoble, perhaps even base, to ask such a self-serving question, suffused as we all are with the notion that the worship of God is supposed to be its own reward. But that's only a risk when we consider the issue from the vantage point of *our* spiritual philosophy - and it seems undeniable in light of the textual evidence that the issue of what the pious get for their religious efforts was a question that did indeed exercise and vex those curious (if not necessarily troubled) ancients for whom its various answers were formulated. In its own way, it is a question all working rabbis (like me) deal with over and over in the course of their, or rather our, professional lives. What's more, I imagine the same must be true for clergymen and women of all faiths.

I have been asked that question a thousand times in a thousand different settings and contexts. Lacking the courage to answer honestly, I usually fall back on some quotation or another from Scripture for my response - as though a verse from the Bible had been what my congregant had been soliciting in the first place. (It wasn't for nothing that the ancient rabbis wrote that when a question is not readily answerable, it is dealt with most efficaciously by burying it under a mountain of Biblical citations.) But even that sort of fancy textual footwork doesn't really even sidestep the question all that effectively because Scripture itself offers two (apparently) mutually exclusive answers of its own. In its own way, the question of whether those two answers are as *truly* antithetical as they appear at first glance or whether they only appear to contradict each other is the subject of this book.

Within the confines and context of the Torah itself, the question is usually answered without actually being asked. Nonetheless, it seems obvious that the various passages that manage to answer it anyway all have some or another version of the same question hiding just behind them. What is the point of fidelity to the covenant? What are the rewards the faithful may expect as recompense for that fidelity? Why should anyone keep the commandments? What is the precise nature of the bargain struck at Sinai between God and the nascent people of Israel? And if what God gets as His part of the bargain is the perpetual worship of Israel, then what exactly is it that the worshippers of Israel may reasonably expect to get from God in return?

The Torah returns over and over to these questions, especially (but not exclusively) in the Book of Deuteronomy. A scholar of the Biblical text would probably wonder why these passages seem grouped in texts that appear to have their origin in one setting and time rather than in another. But that question, fascinating though it would be to consider, will take us too far afield of the topic at hand: I wish to consider the Torah as a finished work, the post-exilic work of well-redacted Jewish genius that exists in our day as a unified, textually verifiable, literary masterpiece of ancient Jewish spirituality.

Of all the passages that attempt to make explicit the reward for fidelity to the commandments, the best known must be the passage from the eleventh chapter of Deuteronomy which the rabbis of classical antiquity designated for liturgical recitation twice daily. There, the idea is a simple one: if the faithful Israelites do all the commandments then the rain will fall, the grass will grow and not only they, but their children as well, can expect to live long lives on the land God promised their ancestors would be theirs.

Other passages appear to be elaborations of the same basic idea. Deuteronomy 28, for example, offers a list merely longer, but not essentially different from the text just cited: the faithful will be blessed in every way (as will their children, their produce and their livestock) and God will grant them political, military, financial and moral superiority over their enemies. Furthermore, this is a permanent offer: even if Israel strays from its obligations, God will always "restore their fortunes and take them back in love" once they set aside their rebelliousness and become obedient again.

Still other texts speak of the possibility of Israel guaranteeing the permanence of this situation by remaining faithful to the commandments of the Torah in the first place. Still, even though the terminology changes from passage to passage, the basic point always remains the same: there are great things that come along with being the beloved people of God, but Israel can only access these marvellous blessings by being faithful to the laws and statutes set down in the Torah. The point of observance, therefore, is to provoke God into granting Israel the widest possible scope of blessing, to make her blessed above all other peoples, even to ward off sickness.

These ideas return over and over again in Deuteronomy. "Keep the commandments ... so that it be good for you and for your children after you," one passage declares, while another responds almost antiphonally "... so that you fear the Lord...and so that you live a long life." Another text is more explicit: if Israel obeys the rules of the Torah and observes them carefully, "then God will love you and bless you and multiply you and bless the fruit of your womb and the fruit of your land, your new grain and wine and oil, the calving of your herd and the lambing of your flock...you shall be blessed above all other peoples; there shall be no sterile male or female among you or among your livestock. The Lord will ward off from you all sickness ...."

Some passages are brief and to the point: "... so that you live and multiply and come to inherit the land ...", "so that you live a long life in the land ...", " ... so that it be good for you and for your descendants forever ...." A different text, however, adds both a financial and a political dimension to the equation: " ... for the Lord your God will bless you ... you shall lend to other nations, but you shall not borrow / you shall rule over many nations, but none shall rule over you."

One passage makes human and animal fertility the crux of the matter: " ... and the Lord will grant you great prosperity in all your undertakings, in the fruit of your womb and the fruit of your animal(s' wombs) and the fruit of the land ...." In turn, another is supremely elegant in the awful simplicity of its *quid pro quo* theology: you must do the bidding of God "so that you live and multiply and that the Lord your God bless you ...."

I've already mentioned that most of these Scriptural passages derive from the Book of Deuteronomy; one passage in Exodus, however, insists that the real reward Israel can expect in return for keeping its side of the covenant is God's help in driving out the indigenous peoples of Canaan. From the vantage point of Biblical chronology, this makes perfect sense: when Israel was still wandering in the wilderness, the reward that could be counted upon to inspire the people the most deeply and effectively was the divine promise of the land itself. Then, once the Israelites were finally positioned to embark on the actual conquest of the land that lay before them - the situation that pertains throughout the Book of Deuteronomy - the text widens its scope to offer not merely possession of the land, but all the marvellous things the land can produce as well.

Another text, itself among the more well-known of such passages, appears at the end of Leviticus, where Scripture counts off the rewards the pious may reasonable expect for all their efforts. Again here, the literary setting is slightly different from the passages cited above, but the actual list of rewards remains the same: rain, prosperity, bountiful crops, political peace, an absence of vicious beasts in the land, military victory over even exceedingly mighty enemies, personal fertility, a successful Temple in Jerusalem (the site is left unnamed in the traditional way of Scriptural passages set before David's conquest of that city) and a deep, ongoing, mutually rewarding partnership with God.

The Psalter, for its part, presents an entirely different picture, one rooted, I think, in the prophetic rather than the priestly experience of the divine.

Passages in the psalms that offer political, meterological, military or agricultural rewards to the pious are very rare, but the Psalter does return again and again to the idea that the ultimate religious experience to which the pious may aspire is intimate, personal communion with God, often expressed specifically as the experience of gazing on the actual (and openly anthropomorphically conceived) image or face of the Deity or of being bathed in His light or, at the very least, as the experience, remarkable in its own right, of hearing His voice.

The seventeenth psalm is typical in that we can see the poet moving smoothly from the assertion that his supplication is guileless (verse 1) to the justification that his feet have followed the path towards God (verse 5) to the ultimate hope that he can reasonably expect, at least someday, to merit the experience of beholding the face of God in a waking state (as opposed to beholding it in the context of a vision or a dream.) That, the Torah declares specifically that it was precisely this experience of beholding God's actual image that set aside Moses from all the other prophets, let alone pious non-prophets, only delineates the chasm of religious experience that divides Torah from Psalter more clearly. I shall return to the seventeenth psalm below.

Some passages within the Book of Psalms specify that this sensory experience of the divine is to be sought specifically within the confines of the Temple, a fact that presumably reflects the fact that the Levitical singers of the Second Temple period, whose hymnal the Psalter was, were not peripatetic wanderers like their (spiritual) ancestors of the pre-exilic period, but rather functionaries who pursued their spirituality within the context of service to the Temple in Jerusalem. Indeed, the fact that the Torah itself takes the distinct traditions about a prophetic sanctuary set up and managed by Moses outside of the camp and a priestly one presided over by Aaron at the very centre of the Israelite camp and makes of them one single sanctuary probably reflects the fact that the spiritual descendants of both the prophets and the priests, their distinct and separate origins notwithstanding, did indeed serve together in the same institution in the day of the final priestly editor of the text. (I will return to this strange feature of the Biblical text below in my epilogue to this book.)

If that was the case, however, then the fact nonetheless remains that these groups didn't coalesce quite to the extent Scripture might be said to have forecast. Instead, they appear to have pursued distinct spiritual paths towards what they probably would have considered the common goal of worshipping of God in the way He wishes to be worshipped.

Thus, when the author of the sixty-third psalm writes about his fervent hope to behold God in His sanctuary, he uses a form of the specifically prophetic word *hazah* to denote the experience of gazing on God, just as did the author of the seventeenth psalm. The rather obscure ending to the eleventh psalm (*yashar yehezu fanêmo*) uses the same verb and must be interpreted, I think, along the lines of the seventeenth and sixty-third psalms as well, especially insofar as it too makes reference specifically (if slightly obscurely) to the divine face.

The twenty-seventh psalm preserves the same connection between the experience of gazing on God and physical presence in the Temple, but refines the idea somewhat: the poet longs to dwell in the Temple permanently not merely (merely!) that he might one day see the divine face, but specifically so that he might gaze (again a form of *hazah*) on the beauty of God. We return below to all these texts and passages.

The eleventh, seventeenth, twenty-seventh and sixty-third psalms are all "David" psalms, but it is not only within psalms ascribed to David that the notion of gazing on God occurs. The forty-second psalm, for example, is ascribed to (one of) the sons of Korach and in it, the poet calls out that his soul thirsts for the living God and asks when it will finally come to pass that he will be able to gaze on the face of God. I suppose one could write off his question as so much extended metaphor, but he does *sound* like he means it and that certainly seems like the logical way to read his poem.

Other psalms offer more oblique references that are only explicable with reference to less-guarded passages in the style of the verses mentioned above.

When the author of the 140th psalm declares, for example, that the upright shall surely dwell in the presence of the divine face, the reference is probably to the same kind of mystical experience held out elsewhere in the Psalter as the appropriate reward for the pious. (Indeed, the opening of the 111th psalm makes specific reference to a smaller conventicle of the upright within a larger congregation that worships God with all their hearts. Might these special people not be those Levites who spent their lives seeking to know God experientially, rather than merely through His service?) Similarly, the reference in the twenty-fourth psalm to a specific circle of people within the author's world who sought the divine face was probably intended to refer specifically to those who cultivated the kind of mystic encounter with the face of God referred to in so many other places in the Psalter. To presume that none of these groups *actually* existed or, even more strangely, that the poets who wrote of them meant their words to bear other than their plain meaning, seems forced to me. They *all* sound like they meant what they said.

I've dwelt on the visual aspect of the kind of divine communion offered by the Psalter, but there are passages that speak of communing with God by hearing His voice rather than by seeing Him or His face. I will return below to this idea, which has its roots in the spirituality of those prophets of antiquity like Elijah whose intimate knowledge of God appears to have been based on the experience of hearing the divine voice rather than on the experience of seeing anything at all. Suffice it here to say that when the author of the thirty-fourth psalm wrote the words "I sought God and He answered me", I think he meant it as literally as the author of the fiftieth psalm did when he produced his definitive *cri de coeur*, "May our God come and be not silent ...."

Moreover, it is also the case that at least some of the ancient poets who specify that the communion they seek with God is to be an essentially auditory experience also stipulate that the place in which they hope to hear this divine voice is precisely within the sacred precincts of the Jerusalem Temple. Thus when the author of the third psalm writes that God answers him from His holy mountain when he calls upon Him to do so, I think he is probably alluding to the specific place in which such mystic communion with God was sought rather than merely saying something theoretical, but vague, about the degree to which anyone who visited old Jerusalem could easily feel the presence of God in that place.

Jewish antiquity produced two great five-part books, Torah and *Tillim*, Pentateuch and Psalter. Each defines the rewards the pious may reasonably expect (and which the cynic will suppose to be the primary motivating force behind their piety) in its own way. As I suggested above, they appear to be mutually exclusive, but all they really are is different. After all, why shouldn't people who devote their spiritual energy to the cultivation of visions of God not enjoy His great blessings of prosperity, fertility or security? What we are talking about, then, is not an either/or kind of spiritual choice, but rather a hierarchy of religious goals and values. No logical believer would decline the blessings of God, after all. But whether the acquisition of those blessings serves as the primary (or secondary or tertiary) focus of a person's spiritual efforts is another question entirely ... and one that has the power to define both the scope and the quality of that individual's religious life. The question is, therefore, not an idle one to be dismissed lightly.

Before I go any further, there is something I must make clear about the nature of my work on the Psalms. The Psalter is an anthology of poems. Some are undoubtedly very old, perhaps even as old as the age of David and his contemporaries. I am not that interested here in the history of the individual poems in the book, however, as much as I am in the book itself. The poems in the Psalter, old and new, were collected into a single work in the post-exilic period by individuals who found them, we can only assume, deeply meaningful. Other hymns must have been excluded, presumably because they failed to meet the anthologizer's criteria for *in*clusion in his book, whatever those criteria specifically might have been. When precisely the book took on its current shape is a question scholars have debated endlessly, but which remains unanswered in any definitive sense. I think a date somewhere in the fourth or third centuries B.C.E. is probably right.

The point here, however, is not to ask who wrote any particular psalm, but to wonder why that poem appears in the Psalter as it was edited and prepared for publication in the post-exilic period and why that *particular* song was deemed acceptable and another poem not. If the Levites were the singers of the old Temple, then what aspect of their spirituality was mirrored in the poems they included in their hymnal? And if, as I am going to posit, these Levites were proponents of a kind of latter-day prophetic Judaism, then what was it about the poetry of the Psalter that appeared to them to endorse or justify that *specific* kind of ancient Jewish spirituality?

Taken as a finished work, the Torah itself, for all its ancient materials and sources, is a product of the post-exilic age as well. From that vantage point, the Psalter is precisely the same: a later work that undoubtedly incorporates a great deal of earlier material. The question I have in both cases, then, is not so much whence that material came - although I'd love to know - but why it was deemed appropriate for the particular book in which it now appears ... and what its inclusion in that work can teach us about the people who included it.

The point of this book is to suggest that the Psalter presents an alternate kind of ancient Jewish religion, the kind that was eventually almost (but *only* almost) overwhelmed and extinguished by the success of rabbinic Judaism and its fundamental (and fundamentalist) assumptions about the unique nature of the Torah as divine revelation. To try to understand what *is* without recourse to what *could have been*, I think, is as pointless as it is ultimately impossible. But this was not a war between two opposing systems of faith I'm imagining: it was far more subtle than that, more of an ever-shifting mix of two things that ended up with a lot more of one constituent element than the other. Could it have been otherwise? That question, as unanswerable as it is fascinating, is at the core of the way I think about my own Jewish identity. I write, then, to offer it as a prism to others through which they may which to focus their own thinking about what Judaism is in our day. But first, a bit of background....

2. What the Chronicler Thought

Put as plainly as possible, I've come to think of the Psalter as a prophetic work *both* because it offers its readers the hope of aspiring to a kind of intimate knowledge of God similar to the kind of communion with the divine experienced by the members of the prophetic caste in ancient Israel *and* because it is filled with oracles that I presume were the substantive results of its authors' experiences of God. What's more, I think that there is an author whose books were included in the Biblical canon who saw it precisely the same way.

We begin with a shadowy figure called the Chronicler. He (or she!) lived a long time ago, probably sometime in the middle of the fourth century B.C.E. and gets his (or her) name from the Book of Chronicles, which he (or she) wrote. (As I've done with the authors of the psalms, I'll continue to write about the Chronicler using masculine pronouns. The Chronicler's actual gender is, of course, unknown.)

Actually, the question of the Chronicler's precise dates has exercised scholars far more seriously than the issue of the author's gender. The problem has been debated forever, but the basic principle is that the book gives the names of nine generations' worth of descendants for Zerubbabel, the leader of the Jewish community in Jerusalem at the time the Second Temple was built. Therefore, since the Temple was rebuilt towards the end of the sixth century, a mid-fourth century date sounds about right. But even if the Chronicler lived before the Book of Psalms received its final form, it still seems reasonable to assume he knew many of its poems from whatever version of the Temple hymnal that *eventually* because our Psalter did exist in his day. It's also entirely possible that the Book of Psalms existed in the Chronicler's day just as it has come down to us.

The Chronicler's book, now divided into two volumes called First and Second Chronicles, is a revision of earlier books of Israelite history in light of the experiences of those who returned from exile in Babylon and their descendants. (The Biblical books of Ezra and Nehemiah were probably intended, either by the same author or a different one, as a kind of appendix to the work.) What all this boils down to is that the Bible presents the history of Israel twice, once (stretching roughly from Deuteronomy through the Book of Kings) told from what is basically an amalgam of pre-exilic and exilic points of view (the exilic material is easily identifiable and is layered over a much larger literary substratum of pre-exilic material) and once, in the Chronicler's book, focused through the prism of Israel's post-exilic experience.

Why is any of this important? It's certainly the case that the Book of Chronicles has inherent importance as a major work of ancient Jewish historiography, but I only introduce the work and its author here because of what the book has to say about the various individuals to whom the psalms of the Psalter are attributed.

There are 150 poems in the Book of Psalms. Many of them appear without attribution, but many others, a majority, have headings that attribute them to specific personalities. Seventy-three psalms, for example, are attributed to King David. Others are attributed to other figures, some famous personalities in their own right like Moses (Psalm 90) or King Solomon (Psalms 72 and 127), others more obscure personalities like Asaph (Psalms 50 and 73-83), Heman (Psalm 88), Ethan (Psalm 89), Jeduthun (Psalms 39, 62 and 77) and the otherwise unnamed sons of Korach (Psalms 42, 44-49, 84, 85, 87 and 88.) Interestingly enough, all of these otherwise unknown personalities (with the exception of Ethan and the sons of Korach) are identified by the Chronicler as prophetic figures, as is King David himself. (Many psalms bear double attribution, as the careful reader will have already noticed. Also, the ascription of the seventy-seventh psalm to Jeduthun is only one way of reading the text of the first verse as it has come down to us.)

Now the Chronicler (at 1 Chronicles 25:1) specifically identifies Asaph, Heman and Jeduthun as men who "prophesied to the accompaniment of lyres, harps and cymbals." Furthermore, the Chronicler specifically gives the number of these three men's descendants as 288, a number strongly reminiscent of the story of the seventy-two elders upon whom God poured out the spirit of prophecy in the days of Moses, the original members - aside from Moses himself - of Israel's prophetic caste. (288 is four times seventy-two.) In other passages, the Chronicler prefers the word seer (Hebrew: *hozeh*) to prophet (*navi'*), describing Heman as a seer at 1 Chronicles 25:5, Asaph as a seer at 2 Chronicles 29:30 and Jeduthun specifically a royal seer (i.e. as a seer connected with the royal court of King David) at 2 Chronicles 35:15. (The Chronicler also tells the story about how one Yahaziel, a member of the Asaphite clan, became a prophet in the time of King Jehoshaphat.)

It is highly significant that none of these individuals (except for King David himself and poor Heman, whom the Book of Kings pauses for a moment to note was, for all his wisdom, still less wise than Solomon) is even mentioned in the pre-exilic work of Israelite history I mentioned above, the work scholars have taken to calling the Deuteronomic History; the Chronicler was apparently specifically interested in providing historical prophetic roles to these men precisely *because* a significant number of the poems included in the Book of Psalms were attributed to them. I presume this was because he perceived their literary oeuvre to be basically prophetic - perhaps "oracular" would be the better word - in nature. (Why no prophetic role was provided for Ethan, whose single psalm should have made him no less reasonable a candidate for *ex post facto* prophetic status than Heman, I can't say. There is some evidence, however that the Chronicler identified Ethan and Jeduthun, perhaps even inadvertently. At any rate, Ethan (whose five references in Chronicles all come before the end of 1 Chronicles 15) and Jeduthun (all but one of whose eleven mentions come after the beginning of 1 Chronicles 16) never appear together in any narrative.)

The case of David is extremely interesting in its own right. The beginning of 1 Chronicles 25, for example, states quite clearly that it was David himself who selected the seers Asaph, Heman and Jeduthun and their hundreds of offspring - both male and female - to be the "trained singers for the Lord."

Of course, that David should have been partial to prophetic figures is part of the larger tradition connecting him to the institution of prophecy. In 1 Chronicles 22, for example, David is portrayed as reporting a prophetic message he received from God to Solomon, then just an "untried youth". Indeed, David is depicted just lines before this passage as a true forerunner of Elijah whose prophetic status received divine confirmation in precisely the same way the Book of Kings, which the Chronicler undoubtedly knew, reported regarding Elijah. One has the sense that if the Chronicler refrained from mimicking the psalmist's portrayal of David as being drawn from the water in the manner of the baby Moses, it was simply because he did not include any birth narrative for David at all. (A later psalmist had no such reticence, however, and used precisely the same word to describe David being "drawn from mighty waters", as Scripture elsewhere uses of Moses being pulled from the river by Pharaoh's daughter.)

The Chronicler doesn't hesitate to acclaim David as a *bona fide* prophet. At 2 Chronicles 8:14, for example, he specifically calls David "a man of God", a term used scores of times throughout Scripture as a technical term denoting a prophet and which he himself uses twice to describe Moses. And, in a famous passage at the beginning of the third chapter of 2 Chronicles, the author actually provides David with the experience of having seen God, an event earlier sources recorded as having been experienced by David's son Solomon not once but twice, but not by David himself.

Of course, the author of Chronicles had firm ground to stand on in describing David as a prophet in that tradition, even in his day, had long connected Samuel's anointing of David as king of Israel with the latter's simultaneous assumption of the mantle of prophecy: "Samuel took the horn of oil and anointed him (i.e. David) in the presence of his brothers; and the spirit of the Lord came over David from that day on ... (1 Samuel 16:13.)" (Why the Chronicler omitted this tradition from his own (admittedly truncated) description of David's anointing by Samuel at 1 Chronicles 11:3, I cannot say.)

Even the version of David's "last words" recorded in 2 Samuel 23 attests to his unqualified self-conception as a prophet of Israel: "The spirit of the Lord has spoken through me / His word has been on my tongue." Solomon also makes the point that God spoke "with His mouth" to his father David, a remark that can only mean that Solomon (or the author of his speech) took David to be an actual prophetic figure who received the word of God directly rather than through the agency of some other prophetic spokesman. As I've already mentioned, the Chronicler goes further than his sources, however, when he notes that God actually appeared to David. The earlier sources leave *that* unsaid, but the Chronicler must have simply, perhaps even inadvertently, assumed that a prophet of David's stature and calibre would naturally have had visual as well as auditory experiences of the divine.

In short, we can certainly agree with the author who wrote that, for his Biblical biographers, David, at least at the end of his life, was above all a prophet. Now, this is hardly a modern idea - an old rabbinic tradition preserved in the Talmud teaches that David was able to compose all the psalms attributed to him (and perhaps the rest as well) because "the Shekhinah - the spirit of God on earth - came over him, whereupon he wrote the songs." Later, Saadia Gaon, the tenth century (C.E.) rabbi revered (among other things) as the father of Jewish philosophy, slightly altered the Talmudic tradition to the effect that David was the editor of the Psalter when he wrote that "the entire psalter is prophecy that David prophesied." And Saadia was not alone. Two centuries later, Abraham Ibn Ezra wrote that he too believed the entire Psalter to have been written under the influence of the Holy Spirit, which is to say, as a work of prophecy rather than of literary creativity. Judging from his comments to Psalm 48:10, Rashi also seems to have taken at least some of the psalmists to have been prophets as well.

In light of all the material assembled above, it seems reasonable to assert that the author of Chronicles, who lived during the period of the Second Temple *and* who obviously had a great deal of presumably inner knowledge of its workings and procedures *and* who knew the Psalter (or some earlier form of it) as the hymnal of the Levitical singers of that Temple, felt it reasonable to portray the authors of the psalms, both the major and even most of the minor figures to whom the various poems in the Psalter are attributed, as prophetic figures because he took the Levitical Temple singers of his day as the latter-day proponents of the kind of spirituality he connected (rightly or wrongly) with the pre-exilic prophets.

Indeed, the Chronicler seems to have felt so certain that the Levites of his own day were the spiritual descendants of the prophets of the First Temple period, that he either intentionally or inadvertently fixed the text of 2 Kings 23:2 ("And the king went up to the Temple along with all the men of Judah and all the inhabitants of Jerusalem and the priests and the prophets and the entire people from young to old ....") to read that the king went up to the Temple in the company of the priests and Levites, almost as though he considered Levite to be the contemporary word for prophet.

There are some interesting conclusions I'd like to draw from all of this, but first I think it might be necessary to introduce some of the pre-exilic prophets in their own setting. They were an odd lot, you see, these prophets of old ....

3. A Different Man

An odd lot, indeed. Scholars - not to mention Sunday School teachers - have traditionally broken them down into two major subgroups: the wandering mystics to whom reference is repeatedly made in the Books of Samuel and the Books of Kings and the great literary figures whose recorded speeches make up the central section of the Hebrew Bible, individuals whose names - Amos, Hosea, Isaiah, Jeremiah, Ezekiel and the like - have become household words in the West. But that distinction is more in the beholder's eye than anywhere within the Scriptural text and corresponds more precisely to the way Western readers have wished to think about religion than to anything Scripture actually says about the prophets of ancient Israel.

Indeed, the fact that the words and oracles of the anonymous peripatetics went (for the most part) unrecorded for future generations while the great speeches of the literary prophets are preserved in the longer or shorter books that bear their famous names is testimony to nothing more profound than the vagaries of literary history - and certainly has nothing to do with the quality of the actual experience of communion with the divine that yielded both the oracles of the wanderers *and* the grand orations of their more famous colleagues. If the nuts and bolts of the prophetic process are absent (for the most part) in the works of the literary prophets, then it seems more cogent to ask why that might be than to assume that their silence means that there was no process at all behind their visions and ecstatic encounters with their supremely communicative God.

Far less well known than the Isaiahs and Jeremiahs, however, are the roving bands of wandering prophets we find mentioned in so many stories about daily life in ancient Israel. We first encounter them on the day Saul ben Kish was anointed king of Israel. Samuel is anxious to conclude his remarks to Saul with a series of simple, highly effective signs that would serve to validate his right to anoint anyone king, so he pulls a prophetic rabbit out of his hat and tells Saul precisely whom he will meet along the road in the course of the coming day. First, he's going to cross paths with two men near the Tomb of Rachel and those men will tell him about the lost sheep he had left home to search for in the first place. Then, at a place called Alon Tabor, he's going to run into three pilgrims on their way to Bethel - and Samuel knows what packages they are going to have in their hands and how much of the contents of which of them they will offer to Saul as a gift to a fellow traveller.

And then, at a place called Givat Ha'elohim, Saul is going to encounter a band of prophets playing lyres, flutes, harps and drums and speaking words of ecstatic prophecy as they make their slow progress down from the high place where they will have just concluded their ritual worship. But meeting up with them is only the beginning. "The spirit of God will then come over you as well," Samuel tells the young Saul, "and you shall become a prophet (or "behave like a prophet" or "utter ecstatic oracles like a prophet"; Hebrew: *mitnabb'ê*) with them and you shall become a different man."

It all happens just as Samuel says it will. Scripture doesn't bother to record the details of Saul's encounters at Rachel's Tomb or Alon Tabor, but when he gets to Givat Ha'elohim, the text becomes precise: Saul sees the band of prophets coming towards him, the spirit of God comes over him and he prophesies in their midst, just as Samuel predicted he would. Unfortunately, the story stops more or less there with the locals being amazed that Saul has apparently given up his putative career as a young gentleman to become an ecstatic prophet and with Saul, now (presumably) the "different man" Samuel said he was going to become, making his way to the shrine in which the prophets had been worshipping just before he had encountered them.

What kind of place was this *bamah*, this shrine? What went on there? The severely deuteronomized author of the Book of Samuel no doubt loathed even having to admit that a man of Samuel's stature could conceivably have spoken of prophets who hung out at a local high-place (for such is the literal meaning of *bamah*) without pausing to express his disgust, but the story merely reports the detail without approving *or* disapproving of its various implications and ramifications. What manner of persons were these prophets? Were they all men or were there women in their ranks? Were they all deeply pious? For that matter, were they all the same thing - or were there gradations and subsects within the prophetic movement, distinctions lost in the blur of centuries that separate us from them?

We encounter this caste of professional prophets - one could almost call it a guild - many times in Scripture and almost each reference offers us some new detail about them. Sometimes, as in the story above, they are portrayed as wanderers, but they are depicted in other passages as belonging to specific places. Moreover, they are often presented as possessing special knowledge of the future (that is, of the will of God), knowledge the reader can only assume came specifically from their experience of the divine - even if Scripture does do its careful best to mask the precise nature of those instances of spiritual communion. Thus, Scripture freely states that it was the *benê hannevi'im* - the circle of local prophets - in both Jericho and Bethel that informed Elisha ben Shaphat of the imminent death of Elijah, Elisha's master. But of the *way* in which they learnt of Elijah's impending demise, Scripture is maddeningly silent.

At least some of the prophets of old Israel lived in disciple circles grouped around a spiritual master - Scripture is particularly informative about the *benê hannevi'im* who were disciples of Elisha's - but others were clearly attached to the royal house and had, at least in a formal sense, the king of the land as their master.

As far as the issue of gender goes, Scriptural passages specifically relating to the prophets as members of fixed or wandering groups do not make reference to female prophets. On the other hand, Scripture mentions the names of several women prophets in other contexts and nowhere is there any specific assertion that these groups were exclusively male. Finally, a wonderful story in the Book of Kings (that, among other things, bears remarkable resemblance to the story the rabbis were to tell centuries later about the miracle of Chanukah) makes it clear that these prophets married and became the parents of children. (For what it's worth, we know that many of the named, literary prophets of Israelite antiquity also married. Indeed, the divine command to Jeremiah *not* to marry in Jerusalem on the eve of its destruction makes it clear that, under happier circumstances, he would have otherwise been permitted, possibly even expected, to take a wife.)

Equally as frustrating as trying to understand much about the nature of ecstatic prophecy in ancient Israel by tracing the history of the prophetic caste is trying to do so by analyzing Scriptural references to the divine spirit which seized the young King Saul and made of him "a different man". Scripture starts off promisingly with the story of Saul assuming the charism of prophecy on the very day of his investiture as king of Israel - just as it would eventually say of David as well - then stops short and starts to use the phrase "spirit of God" as a mere synonym for charisma or even mental wellbeing, precisely as it is used elsewhere in the Biblical text regarding Samson, Jephthah and other ancient non-prophetic personalities.

On the other hand, there is something tantalizing about the way this same spirit of God is described when it comes over *bona fide* prophets. Obadiah, the steward of King Ahab's palace and great friend of the royal prophets, seemed to think this divine spirit could transport the prophet over great distances; indeed, the prophets of Jericho themselves are heard to speak to Elisha in such a way that we can reasonably conclude that they thought that someone truly possessed of the spirit could fly. And then there's the detail given in the Book of Kings to the effect that Elijah, once possessed of the spirit of God, could outrun a horse-drawn chariot.

There is even something provocative about the language Scripture uses to describe the way in which the divine spirit comes over a prophet. It doesn't just awaken within him. It fills him with strength. It overwhelms him. It falls on him. It comes mightily upon him. It envelops him like a garment. It descends upon him and then rests on him like the fog of God rested on Sinai when the entire people heard His voice - that is, when for one exquisite moment the entire nation became, not a nation of priests after all, but one of prophets.

But even if Scripture is vague about the spiritual activities of the prophetic caste, it does make it clear that there was something magical - and compulsory, if not quite compulsive - about the ecstatic experience. One story especially interesting in this regard has to do with David's escape from Saul, now almost wholly mad and seized with paranoid (but not entirely unjustified) loathing of the man he sees as his own son's greatest rival for the throne of Israel. David escapes to Ramah, where he finds Samuel, and together the two of them go to a place called Naioth. Saul hears where they are and sends messengers to seize David.

The messengers come to Naioth and find the prophets in the throes of ecstatic experience with Samuel at their head and they - the messengers sent to arrest David - begin to prophesy as well. Then, *"when Saul was told about this, he sent other messengers, but they too spoke in ecstasy. Saul sent a third group of messengers, but they also spoke in ecstasy. So he himself went to Ramah. When he came to the great cistern at Secu, he asked "Where are Samuel and David?" and was told that they were at Naioth in Ramah. He was on his way there, to Naioth in Ramah, when the spirit of God came upon him too; and he walked on, speaking in ecstasy, until he reached Naioth in Ramah. Then he too stripped off his clothes and he too spoke in ecstasy before Samuel; and he lay naked all that day and all night ...."*

Does the word "too" mean that the prophetic experience was generally undertaken in the nude? Does the reference to Saul lying on the ground mean that the essence of the prophetic experience was achieved in a self-induced trance-state that left the body immobilized for as long as it lasted? It seems reasonable to imagine that this was indeed the case, at least occasionally, but other Biblical passages suggest that the peak experience was one of waking communion with the divine. (Scripture does preserve at least one text that refers to Levites, at least under some unspecified circumstances, as being unable to recognize their own parents, children or siblings!) Perhaps different individuals experienced prophecy in different ways ... some awake, some asleep, some entranced, some wholly aware, some with their clothes on and others with them off.

But I fear we may have wandered a bit too far afield of my original question, to which I now return with a new formulation: is there evidence, I now wish to ask, that the pre-exilic prophets of Israel pioneered a kind of experiential, mystic communion with God that involved sensual contact with God of the kind promised in the Psalter as the ultimate reward for the pious? That, more than anything else, is the crux of the matter I wish to consider ....

4. Seeing God

The earliest extra-Pentateuchal historical personality we hear declaring unequivocally that he saw the God of Israel is Michaihu ben Yimlah, a little known prophet who was a contemporary of Elijah's.

In the only story that features him, this Michaihu is portrayed as the mediator in a dispute between King Ahab of the northern kingdom of Israel and King Jehoshaphat of Judah in the south. The former is trying to enlist the aid of the latter in a proposed war against the king of Aram over the city of Ramot Gilead which the king of Aram had previously seized from Ahab. The prudent Jehoshaphat, however, is not interested in taking any chances - he agrees to participate in the campaign, but asks for an oracle of confirmation just to make sure that his decision was the right one.

King Ahab, it turns out, has a palace full of prophets - four hundred or so - and so he puts the question to them. His question is simple enough - "Shall I go up against Ramot Gilead or shall I desist?" - and their answer is immediate and to the point: "Go against it, for God shall deliver it into the hand of the king."

Perhaps it's the odd immediacy of the response, or perhaps it's the uncanny unanimity of all four hundred prophets speaking with one voice, but for whatever reason, Jehoshaphat requires a second opinion and asks if there might be another prophet present through whom the oracle might be confirmed. Reluctantly ("for I loathe him because he only forecasts doom for me ..."), Ahab produces Michaihu ben Yimlah, who, to Ahab's surprise, offers a prophecy no less encouraging than the other prophets. Now the Biblical text shows some keen insight into human nature: just as Jehoshaphat had been unable to accept the word of the four hundred at face value, so now is Ahab unable to accept the prophecy of Michaihu.

At this point, we follow the narrative more closely:

And the king said to him (i.e. to Michaihu), *"How many times do I have to adjure you to speak only truth to me in the name of the Lord?" And he replied, "I see Israel scattered on the mountains like so many sheep without a shepherd. The Lord said, 'They have no masters; let each man return to his home in peace.'" The King of Israel then said to Jehoshaphat, "Did I not say to you that he would not prophesy good for me, but rather evil?" He* (Michaihu) *then said, "Therefore hear the word of the Lord. I have seen the Lord seated on His throne and the entire heavenly host stood in attendance, some to the right and some to the left."*

The story goes on to explain that Michaihu learned in heaven that the prophetic spirit stimulating the four hundred was a false one sent by God Himself to fool King Ahab. The exquisite irony is that Ahab, finally presented with the truth, ignores it, goes up against Ramot Gilead anyway and is killed.

In some ways, this is a typical story of ancient Israel, but what sets it apart is that Michaihu is the first historically datable individual we hear saying aloud that he saw the God of Israel. The word the text uses for "to see" is the stark, uncompromising Hebrew *ra'iti*, unambiguous, defiant and utterly frank. The word used of the Lord is the ineffable, personal name of God, leaving no room for misunderstanding or confusion. As I'll discuss in detail below, Scripture says that God stood before the boy Samuel and appeared to David and Solomon generations earlier - but, for what it's worth, neither Samuel, David *nor* Solomon is cited as saying either openly or unambiguously that he saw God and Michaihu is.

This Michaihu, about whom nothing else of any importance is known, had many successors, although there is no particular reason to assume that he himself was the originator of the school of prophetic endeavour that centred on the experience of visual communion with God. Just to the contrary - the impression given by Scripture is that he was *not* a figure of special importance, simply one prophet among many working at the court of Ahab.

In passages set in the middle of the eighth century B.C.E., for example, we read of similar experiences that befell both Amos and Isaiah, the latter precisely in the context of his inaugural prophetic vision. There, the imagery is even richer, as the author describes the panoply of celestial beings that surround the divine throne as well as the divine image seated upon it.

Why these visual images were cultivated is a question that cannot be answered with satisfaction over the long centuries that divide us from these ancient people. Certainly, the notion of a visual experience of God must have had an edge of practicality over a merely auditory one because of the question of initiative: just as we can more easily control who may hear us than who may see us, so do we get the impression that God speaks to His prophets when He wishes - but that the prophet who achieves visual communion with God bears some higher level of responsibility for having provoked the experience. On the other hand, the psalms are filled with hymns designed to provoke or trigger divine speech as well as the experience of seeing God - so perhaps the analogy to human relationships is less apt than one would ordinarily think. Also, there is the added intimacy of the visual experience to consider - even today, seeing, not hearing, is believing. I suppose that whether a prophet had visual or aural prophetic experiences must have depended to a great extent on whether his own prior conception of God could allow for such an experience, with those prophets who lived and worked within the Biblical tradition of an anthropomorphic Deity able to cultivate visual experiences of the godhead and those who continued the equally hoary tradition of conceiving of God solely as an invisible Deity able to experience only the kind of experiences that corresponded to their notion of an intelligent and communicative but ultimately formless God who could be heard but never seen.

What inner reasons would have brought one prophet to conceive of God in one way and another in the other way is no doubt a deeply personal matter: we can only hypothesize as to the many factors that must have gone into the determination of such a profound aspect of an individual's perceptive nature, much in the same way any modern's conception of God is rooted in a multitude of factors, only some of which have anything direct or obvious to do with that person's religious life or beliefs.

The point is that those prophets who believed that God manifests Himself in an anthropomorphic shape to His human devotees cultivated the visual experience, while those who believed in an amorphic godhead chose to cultivate auditory, intellectual communion with God. But Michaihu, Amos and Isaiah were only the beginning ....

In a class all by themselves are the visions of the prophet

Ezekiel ben Buzi. As a Temple priest banished to Babylon with the first wave of exile during the first decade of the sixth century, Ezekiel was no doubt well-schooled in the varieties of prophetic experience. His description of his experiences on the River Kebar are, perhaps, the most famous part of his entire prophetic oeuvre, but of that long passage, the most relevant verses are the ones that conclude the first chapter of the prophet's book. Ezekiel describes an extraordinary vision, one of surpassing strangeness and beauty, which is crowned with a vision of God Himself. First he describes the weird animals that support the divine throne, then he turns to that which he saw over their heads:

Above the expanse over their heads was the semblance of a throne, in appearance like sapphire; and on top, upon this semblance of a throne, there was the semblance of a human form. From what appeared as his loins up, I saw a gleam as of amber - what looked like a fire encased in a frame - and from what appeared as his loins down, I saw what looked like fire. There was a radiance all about him. Like the appearance of the bow which shines in the clouds on a day of rain, such was the appearance of the surrounding radiance. That was the appearance of the semblance of the Glory of the Lord. When I beheld it, I flung myself down on my face. And I heard the voice of someone speaking ...

Despite the artful dodges around saying precisely that he saw what he more or less frankly admits to his readers that he did see, the fact seems undeniable that Ezekiel had an experience similar in nature and result to that which Michaihu and Isaiah experienced before him. And it wasn't only in the context of that first prophetic experience that Ezekiel managed to see what he called the Glory of God. He saw it again in a vision in which he saw the presence of God clearing out of the Temple just before its destruction by the hordes of Babylon and then again in a vision of the future restoration of the Holy City in which he saw the divine presence - he specifically notes that this was precisely the same image as the one he saw on the banks on the Kebar - returning to the sacred mountain.

The entire Biblical age was an age of prophecy, from the very beginning until the very end. By common consensus, the last book of the Hebrew Bible to have been composed was the Book of Daniel - or at least its final chapters - which makes unmistakable if obscure reference to a variety of incidents that took place in the first quarter of the second century B.C.E. in pre-Maccabean and

Maccabean Palestine. Yet even in the final throes of Biblical creativity, we read of experiences that the author of Daniel had which put him directly in the line of visual prophets stretching from the early days of the split monarchy into the very latest days of the Biblical age. True, Daniel's Ancient of Days, seated on his throne of fire with His snowy white robe and hair like lamb's wool, is not precisely the same godhead described by Ezekiel and the others. Still, the point is not that God changes outfits every couple of centuries, but simply that different individuals perceive God in very different ways ....

5. And Hearing His Voice

Contemporary with Michaihu, but cut from very different cloth, was Ahab's great protagonist, Elijah. Freely described as the leader of the prophetic movement in his generation, Elijah is depicted as a strange package of things - part wonder worker, part prognosticator, part divine spokesperson and part priest. There are many stories and story fragments I could present to you, but one specific story - one of the two most famous of them all, as it happens - seems especially relevant for me to analyze at this juncture.

This particular story begins with Elijah, terrified by Queen Jezebel's threat to kill him, fleeing to the south and stopping about a day's journey beyond Beersheba. There, an angel comes to him with some flat cakes and a pitcher of water, urging him to continue his journey once he takes some sustenance. He does continue and finally arrives at Mount Sinai, where he tarries just like Moses for forty days and nights. He sets up temporary residence in a cave, but he doesn't forget the reason he fled in the first place and when the word of God comes to him, asking, "Why are you here, Elijah?", Elijah answers a bit dramatically that he is the only one of God's prophets left alive and that he is there for the express purpose of saving his own life before Jezebel's henchmen get to him too. "Come out," God calls to him as He fades back into the third person within the context of His own narrative, "and stand on the mountain before the Lord."

Just as Moses was allowed (at least according to one story) to experience the passing of God while standing on (or rather, within) a rock, so was Elijah able to experience God while standing on a mountain crag. "*And lo, the Lord passed by,*" the text begins. "*There was a great and mighty wind, splitting mountains and shattering rocks by the power of the Lord, but the Lord was not in the wind.*

After the wind - an earthquake, but the Lord was not in the earthquake. After the earthquake - fire, but the Lord was not in the fire. And after the fire - a voice of thin silence."

This was the height of Elijah's experience, for the thin silence was the voice of God. What the sound of silence is seems obvious - it can only be the voice you hear within, the voice within your mind or within your consciousness, the voice you hear through the intellect rather than through your ears. I think the Bible is telling us that Elijah experienced the presence of God intellectually or perhaps aurally (if that is the right word to describe the experience of hearing silence), but certainly not visually.

Indeed, in a certain sense, Elijah stands as a giant within the long line of prophets who heard but did not see. Now it's hardly coincidental, I think, that the vast majority of prophets whose words are preserved within Scripture spoke or wrote exclusively of what they heard God say rather than of their experiences gazing on Him. Of course, aural experience is far more informational in nature than its visual counterpart and so lends itself more readily to one particular aspect of the prophetic calling, but it is also worth remembering that it is we who have allowed ourselves to determine which aspect of the spirituality of the ancient prophets constituted the "real" part of their work and which part was its ancillary, less important aspect.

In other words, the fact that all the literary prophets of Israel heard the voice of God and that many of them heard exclusively has led us to conclude that hearing must have been at the centre of the prophetic experience despite the fact that we have no real basis for thinking that other than our own presuppositions about religion and the role God tends to play in the lives of human beings.

Perhaps it is the fact that the experience of hearing God is generally understood to be involuntary (in that God speaks to whom He wishes when He wishes about whatever He wishes), while the visual experience is generally assumed to be sought by the one doing the seeing discouraged the prophets of Israel from describing their visual experiences of God in detail. (Ezekiel's elaborate explanation of how the vision of God was thrust upon him unawares almost seems too strongly stated and could well be the exception that proves the rule.) At any rate, some prophets came out and said that their God could not be seen, as for instance the prophet whose exclamation, "To whom can one compare God; what shape could one ascribe to Him?" is preserved in the Book of Isaiah. Others, we can only assume, felt the same way and found their stance so self-evident as to make it unnecessary to say so formally.

In the end, prophecy has to do with the experience of intense and intimate communion with God. Some prophets interpreted that intimacy visually, while others (bound, perhaps, by prior beliefs and dogmas) interpreted that same experience aurally. Having had the experience once, I suppose it must have been natural to cultivate it a second and third time within the same sensual framework in which a given prophet had already lived through it. Thus grew up different kinds of prophets ... but the experiences of communion with God that rest behind and beyond and beneath both - at least when divested of the interpretations they are forced to acquire when we insist on focusing them through the prism of human sensory perception - must have been quite the same.

And so there appear to have been two schools of prophecy in ancient times, one which promised visual communion with God and one which taught that the best a terrestrial could hope for was hearing His voice. Even calling them separate schools is probably misleading, however. They were different in style and in experiential texture, to be sure. But the difference between them was, in the end, one of style more than of substance. At any rate, both were *bona fide* prophetic stances which are reflected both in the books of the prophets and in the untitled five-part work we call the Psalms. More to the point, they are both valid, both ancient, both totally and historically authentic. And both are as equally feasible - at least in theory - today as they were back when such things were deemed the ordinary stuff of religion, not its exotic shadow ... and certainly not its demented twin.

6. What We Could Have Been

How did the ancients learn to see God? King Uzziah, David's great-great-great-great-great-great-great-great grandson, seems to have taken lessons from a certain Zachariah in how to do just that and the Chronicler reports that God so enjoyed the experience, presumably the experience of being seen by the king, that he granted him special prosperity as a result. Unfortunately, however, the authors of the various psalms leave their techniques, at least for the most part, as undisclosed as the methods of the king's mystic tutor were left unreported by the Chronicler. But among the many texts within the Psalter that speak of seeking God (many of which express the idea with the same verb used by the Chronicler to denote Uzziah's successful quest for visual communion with God), there are more than a few that offer some tantalizing suggestions regarding the road at least some ancients travelled to that august end.

The twenty-seventh psalm, for example, suggests that the act of seeking God took place within the precincts of the Temple itself. The twenty-second psalm adds the possibility that the experience was at least sometimes cultivated in the context of a sacred meal of some sort. Other texts add other possible aspects of the experience. In turn, the sixty-ninth and seventieth psalms confirm what the larger context of the Psalter suggested all along: that the experience was cultivated in the context of hymn singing or chanting and of the search for intense feelings of inner joy.

Other passages are more obscure. Does the reference to Jacob in the twenty-fourth psalm tell us, for example, that Jacob was the patriarch deemed to be the father of the mystic quest for visual communion with God? It would make sense given his experiences at Peniel, a place specifically named by Jacob in honour of his having had precisely that experience in that specific place. (Peniel, at any rate, does indeed mean "face of God" and Jacob, father of Levi, would have made the ideal eponymous ancestor of subsequent generations of Levitical mystic seekers.) The context in the Psalter, however, is not sufficiently fleshed out to permit any conclusive thoughts on the matter, although I wonder if there isn't some sort of corroboration of the idea in the slightly obscure rabbinic tradition that tries to whittle down the number of psalms in the Psalter from 150 to 147, the precise number Scripture gives as the number of years of Jacob's life. (The context makes this connection clear, thereby making it at least possible that the tradition is based on its author's *wish* to come up with that number rather than his conviction that there actually were 147 poems in the book. But what if there really were 147 poems in the original work? Could its editor have been inspired by the degree to which Jacob was revered in his, the editor's, own circles as the father of their particular brand of mystic spirituality?)

Was there a messianic element to the larger undertaking, as the tenth verse of the eighty-fourth psalm might suggest, or merely a royal one? And even if the original author's intent was to connect the search for a vision of God with the experience of gazing on the king, then how did the Levites in the post-exilic, kingless period understand that concept to apply to their own mystic endeavours?

Are all the references in the Psalter to the face of God somehow connected with this Levitical mysticism of the post-exilic age? Surely, for example, one can read the reference to God's face at the end of the ninth psalm without recourse to anything but the literal (i.e. non-mystical) meaning of the text. In a similar category are the references to the theme of *hastarat panim* ("the hiding of the [divine] face") in many different psalms: can these not be taken simply as references to the withdrawal of divine intervention in the world as a punishment for human intransigence and sinfulness? On the other hand, other references to the divine face seem to require interpretation as part of the larger complex of ideas surrounding the search for visual communion with God. The regular references to the light of the divine face, for example, suggest that the actual peak experience of gazing on the Deity was somehow accomplished in a burst of some sort of intense light, but whether that light was focused from without or generated from within cannot be easily deduced from the texts as they have come down to us.

What kind of experience lies just behind the reference in the twenty-first verse of the thirty-first psalm to the *yerê'im* ("the God-fearers") being hidden within the secret folds of the divine face? To the references elsewhere to the *yesharim* ("the righteous") dwelling (the Hebrew could also mean simply sitting) with the divine face? To the psalmist rising at midnight to supplicate before the divine face? To people called "servants of God" gathering together in the Temple court at midnight?

And what did the proponents of this mystical experience call themselves? Seers? Prophets? The Humble Ones? The Seekers of God? The Seekers of the Divine Face? The Upright? The Pious? The God-Fearers? The Righteous? The Servants of God? All these names can be reasonably proposed and buttressed by different verses from the Book of Psalms. But which of them is correct - or if some of them are or if they all are - is not something the textual evidence allows us to say with certainty.

Furthermore, what are the wider implications of the fact that not all the psalms refer to this kind of mystic communion? Are we to conclude that not all the Levites were initiates into this particular kind of religious experience? Or perhaps that private conventicles of mystics existed within the Temple hierarchy and staff to which some were admitted and others excluded? Or would the more logical conclusion simply be that the Levites led complex religious lives in the warp and woof of which the quest for visual or auditory communion with God was only one aspect among many? Or is the Psalter simply a hymnal that contains poetry rooted in a variety of ancient experiences of God, not all of which were features of the spiritual lives of the final editors and redactors of the book?

The answers to all of these questions are lost in the past. Even unanswered, however, they create a clear sense that the Psalter provided a literary counterpart to the priestly spirituality of the Torah, a counterpart rooted instead in the prophetic experience. Indeed, there are more than a few passages in the Book of Psalms that refer *specifically* to their authors' prophetic experiences. How else can we interpret the account offered by the author of the eighty-ninth psalm, for example, of how the substance of God's ancient oracle to the prophet Nathan was confirmed in a prophetic vision (Hebrew: *ḥazon*) revealed to an unidentified group of mystics the author calls God's pious - precisely the term used elsewhere in the Psalter to refer to the mystic poets themselves? Or, to use an even bolder example, how else may we explain the plaintive plea of the author of the fifty-first psalm that God not deprive him of the holy spirit - that breath of divine presence we know the ancients believed to function at the creative core of the prophetic experience? Or the willingness of the author of the poem that appears elsewhere in the Psalter as the second halves of both the sixtieth and the 108th psalms to introduce an otherwise unknown divine oracle with the unambiguous words, "God spoke (these words) in His sanctuary ..."? And then there is the repeated use of the Hebrew verb *darash* to characterize the poets' quest for God, a term that dozens of Biblical texts reveal has its roots specifically in the cultivation of communicative communion with the divine in the context of prophesy ....

But there's another more pointed question resting beneath all this data: since the Psalter undoubtedly received its final literary form in the post-exilic period, we may certainly wonder what the precise literary relationship between the Torah and the Psalter might be. They are, after all, parallel works in a variety of ways: their five-book structure, their strange mix of first and third person material, their internally inconsistent editorial traits, their unselfconscious presentation of the same material in parallel passages and their mixture of priestly and prophetic passages, albeit with very different emphases, all suggest that the later work was edited to resemble, at least formally, the earlier. But which was which cannot be determined conclusively, I don't think, from the evidence at hand. Does the fact that the actual division of the Psalter into five parts appears both artificial and arbitrary suggest that it is the later work? Or is that division executed in an *entirely* cogent way based on secrets of literary provenance that history has effectively hidden from us? (And what, we may also ask, are we to make of the fact that so many post-exilic works - the Torah, the Book of Psalms, the so-called Deuteronomic History, the Chronicler's work (if we follow the suggestions of some scholars and consider the first nine chapters to be a book of genealogies unto itself and include the books of Ezra and Nehemiah), the collection of short scrolls known as *megillot*, even the books of Proverbs and Daniel - are in five parts as well? Were all these works consciously created in five parts for some polemical or doctrinal reason we now longer understand? Or was there another reason?)

For us modern readers, the Psalter is too often marginalized (or dismissed entirely) as a book of old poems printed in the back of the Bible. It is my conviction, however, that a profound understanding both of Israelite religion and of Judaism (or rather, Judah-ism) can only develop from a clear sense of the precise, subtle differences between the various spiritual paths trodden by our spiritual ancestors, one of which paths is clearly the neo-prophetism of the Psalter.

Israel became a kingdom of priests not because it couldn't have become a kingdom of prophets, but because that is the way history ended up working out. But the prophets of ancient Israel were the forebears of the Jewish people in no less real a way than were the priests - and a good deal of what Judaism and Jewish spirituality are today is what they were first. Trying to imagine a less priestly, more prophetic (and severely less deuteronomic) Judaism is a difficult exercise this long after the fact. Still, the reason we study the books of the ancients in the first place is to see what we are by identifying clearly what we could have been. In that quest, the Psalms have become my guide.

7. Asleep in the Temple

And so we turn to the question of our own spirituality. I think it's legitimate to ask, after all, what all this can eventually have to do with us. Are we doomed by the vicissitudes of history to be priests rather than prophets? Must the reward we earn with a lifetime of prayer and ritual observance be rain and fertile herds rather than the experience of gazing on God or hearing His voice? To put it differently: are we the products of our own past or its servants? Or are the records of the past merely there for us to use as foundation stones to support whatever kind of spiritual home we can (or rather, dare) build upon them?

In every post-Biblical generation, there have been individuals who have dreamt of recapturing the prophetic experience of knowing God not merely by reading about Him in books, even in sacred ones, but by seeing His face and by hearing His voice. These are the men and women whose stories make up the history of Jewish mysticism.

For the most part, we claim to revere these individuals as pioneers of Jewish spirituality. But the reality is far removed from the worshipful lip-service we serve up when formally asked how we feel about their work *or* their spirituality - and the truth is that we are so accustomed to treating the Biblical passages that describe the prophetic experience of knowing God as extended metaphors that it seems almost blasphemous to ask if it might not be at least *as* reasonable to take them literally. In the end, it's a confusing set of values we espouse: we personally like our deities invisible and silent, but few of us (I think, I hope) would be willing to dismiss the authors of the various Biblical accounts that preserve eye-witness testimony to this kind of religious experience as charlatans or delusional schizophrenics in the same way we would do just that (or worse) to someone coming as naked as Isaiah to, say, a shopping mall to announce in public (not only) his experience of the living God, but the precise message that God bid him bear to the people of his place.

Yet, despite the best efforts of countless apologists (of all religious and denominational hues and stripes) to argue just to the contrary, there isn't the slightest literary, logical or historical reason to dismiss the Biblical accounts of individuals who knew God in a visceral, utterly sensual way as poetry or metaphor. And so we are led (slightly) innocently into a conundrum of the most maddening insolubility: either denounce (and dismiss and deride and degrade) the words of Scripture as the product of overactive imaginations and the experiences behind them as hallucination and self-induced (and deeply self-referential and self-serving, if not necessarily self-conscious) fantasy - or else accept the possibility of knowing God in the sensual way pioneered by the prophets of old as at least theoretically plausible. Even in our day. Even by ordinary people whose only qualification for the job is the will to know God.

Although the pre-exilic *benê nevi'im* - the peripatetic ecstatics and the fixed-location disciple circles and the platoons of court prophets and the like - appear to have engaged in many different procedures and rituals to induce the trance state in which they could experience the sensually perceptible presence of God, the ancients liked to tell how the greatness of the truly great among the prophets lay in the fact that they did nothing at all to see or hear God, that He chose them and came to them all on His own. This, rather than any real distinction of status or experience, is what makes some of the prophets read differently than others in our sacred texts.

Thus we read that Moses was out mucking around after his father-in-law's sheep when he was suddenly drawn to the spot at which God revealed Himself to him, while Samuel was asleep in the temple at Shiloh, Jeremiah was a boy wandering about in an almost grove, Amos was a lad tending his father's sheep and sycamore trees and Ezekiel was out for a stroll by the banks of a river when they had their initial prophetic experiences. It must have pleased the humble among the prophets to imagine that the most prominent of them earned the right to their fame and prestige precisely by being a breed apart, men (and women!) of God not merely by virtue of the success of their own efforts, but by dint of divine election.

Whether these stories reflected historical reality or were just so many worshipful tales told by later generations about their distant forebears, I don't know. But, as I've already said, I'm not that interested in surveying the great speeches of the prominent individuals whose words form the bulk of the prophetic books of the Bible and trying to guess from their form or content what manner of individual those specific prophets were. Instead, my interest lies principally in the anonymous nobodies who made up the rank and file of the prophetic caste in pre-exilic times and, especially, in the post-exilic Levites who, I believe, stepped into their shoes. It is they, not the Isaiahs or the Jeremiahs - at least as they are portrayed in the Bible - who hold open the possibility of emulation, even this long after the fact. It is they who sought God and found Him and knew Him. And it is they who call to me from their ancient graves and ask to be heard. In their own right. And, if by nothing else, than by virtue of the success of their spiritual endeavours.

I want to analyze some passages from the Psalter that I think shed light on the whole neo-prophetic phenomenon in post-exilic Judah, but first it might be instructive to consider the story the ancients told about the night Samuel ben Elkanah became a prophet in Israel.

It appears to have been widely believed in ancient times that prophecy only really got off the ground in the days of King David, who lived sometime around the end of the eleventh or the beginning of the tenth centuries B.C.E.

Samuel was an older contemporary of David and the story of his investiture as a prophet begins with the remark that back in the days of the Shiloh sanctuary (which was destroyed in Samuel's day and eventually replaced by the Temple Solomon built in Jerusalem), it was very uncommon to hear God speak because prophecy was not widespread. (Indeed, it was not until the time of King Jehoshaphat, David's great-great-great-grandson, that Michaihu reported that he actually achieved visual communion with God, so it sounds about right for the author to say that in these early stages of the prophetic movement, *even* auditory communion with the divine realm was rarely achieved. This is somehow connected to the author's comment only a few chapters later to the effect that even the word "prophet" itself wasn't in common use at this time and that Samuel himself was widely known rather as a seer, a sort of pre-prophetic figure whose job, presumably among other things, appears to have consisted of work on the order of telepathically - if that's the right word - locating other people's lost animals.)

At any event, Samuel was a kind of apprentice lad to Eli, the chief priest at Shiloh at that time and the father of two larcenous, lecherous louts whose reputation did Eli no good at all. But Eli was free not to care too much about his sons' criminality (or so he thought - his first mistake!) because he had a wonderful, pious disciple in the young Samuel. Indeed, just as the Torah would eventually suggest regarding the boy Joshua, Scripture insists that Samuel actually spent his nights sleeping in the innermost sanctum of the Shiloh sanctuary "where the Ark of God was." And it was in that place late one night that the word of God, rare though it may have been in that day, came to the man Scripture would eventually consider to be (if not quite formally to name as) the father of Israelite prophecy.

The story is a famous one with many parallels among the stories of many nations, but there's also something peculiarly Jewish about the tale the way its told in Scripture. God calls to Samuel, who replies (like Abraham, Jacob and Moses before him): *hinêni*, here I am. Except that, missing the point entirely, Samuel thinks it's Eli who's called him. Eli suggests Samuel must have been dreaming and sends him back to bed. Then the same thing happens a second time. And then a third.

By this time, Eli has seized the point and when Samuel comes to him that third time and says that he heard him - Eli - calling, Eli tells him to go lie down again and wait. If he hears himself being called again, Eli advises, Samuel is to say the words "Speak, Lord, for your servant is listening."

It works like a charm. Samuel goes back to bed, God calls on him a fourth time, Samuel responds more or less as Eli had bidden him and God proceeds to speak to him, telling him (more than slightly ironically) about the awful way He is planning to annihilate the house of Eli because of the wretched behaviour of Eli's villainous sons. (There's a nice psychological touch to the story in that Samuel appears willing only to trust his mentor to a point and responds to the call with the words "Speak, for your servant is listening" without calling on God by name as Eli had specifically told him to. He may have been taking the role of the good son in Eli's life, but even Samuel had a little trouble following his master's instructions precisely.)

The story is a good one on any level, but there's something else here worth considering. The first three times God tries to get Samuel's attention, He merely calls out to him. The third time, however, the text makes a point of saying that something else happened. "God then came and stood right there," the text says as boldly as it knows how, adding that God called out Samuel's name twice this time - I'll return to this point below - and that this apparently did the trick: the combination of Eli's instructions, the (presumably) palpable ambience of divine presence and the repetition of Samuel's name finally made him aware of that which had eluded him previously: that he was in the presence of God not merely in the theoretical, theological sense, but in the actual, empirical, practical sense as well. As Scripture says elsewhere about Saul, Samuel had become another man.

Can moderns learn anything from this story about hearing the word of God? Even though it's clearly one of those stories about the greats that the ancients no doubt liked to tell as a way of buttressing their faith in the efficacy of their own brand of Israelite religion, there's also a lot here for the latter-day reader.

First of all, the text specifically notes that Samuel hadn't ever heard the voice of God, much less seen Him before this day. Yet, he was hardly new to religion: he wasn't only a Temple servant among many (even if he appears to have been Eli's private amanuensis), but he lived in the Shiloh sanctuary and was awarded what must have been the terrific honour of actually being permitted to sleep in the presence of the Ark of God. The picture here is of a boy devoted day and night to the worship of God - but who was completely unprepared actually to experience the presence of God in his life in an idiosyncratic, private, personal way.

That aspect of the story hits home especially hard, I think - for of how many of us could the same not be said? We spend our lives *doing* religion rather than worshipping God, performing the appropriate rituals at the appropriate, foreordained times, reciting prayers other people wrote according to schedules yet other people specified as proper, refusing to feel even slightly failed in our spiritual lives because God never commands us personally to do anything at all, let alone come to us in the night and call us by name.

In other words, we are all Samuel, some of us practically sleeping in our synagogues in the shadow of the Arks of the Law that grace their sanctuaries and others of us more distant. But when Scripture remarks of Samuel that this all happened "before he knew God", it means what it says. He knew the rules. He knew the procedures. He served his master well and received, we can only suppose, the appropriate rewards. But he didn't know God because, as the verse continues, God had never actually spoken to him directly before. And what kind of conversation can you have with someone who isn't speaking back? Really!

The text itself speaks volumes, if subtle ones. The first time God calls to Samuel, the text merely says that He called out to him without saying precisely what He said. The second time, the text relates that God specifically called his name out, "Samuel!" When the text relates how God called to Samuel a third time, it again fails to say precisely what He said, but then, the fourth and final time, it says explicitly that He called to him by calling out Samuel's name twice "as before", which presumably means that He had called out "Samuel, Samuel" the third time as well, since the second time He had only called his name out once. But that fourth time, "the Lord came and stood before him" ....

From this progression, I learn that seeing, ultimately, is believing. And hearing can be believing too, but only if one stays tuned in to the station long enough to hear the end of the song. When God called Samuel by name, he mistook the voice of God for his master's. But when God called him by his name twice, something in his deep recollective consciousness was awakened: Samuel was an Ephraimite, as Joshua (who was to Moses as Samuel was to Eli) had been before him. Now Ephraim, the son of Joseph, was the grandson of Jacob - and Samuel no doubt knew the story of Jacob's life, how God appeared to him "in a night vision" at Beersheva as he took his children down to Egypt and called "Jacob, Jacob" to him, and how Jacob answered *hinêni*. In other words, when Samuel was listening with his ears, he missed the point entirely. But when he listened with his heart to the atavistic memories buried deep within its innermost chambers, he heard a lot more. But it wasn't until God stood before him as a physically real, absolutely existent image before his eyes (as Radak paraphrases our text) that he truly knew the God he had previously served but not really known at all.

Finally, Scripture makes a special point of mentioning that Eli was a very old man when this story takes place, a man whose eyes had already begun to dim and who could therefore hardly see. He was a lot of things this Eli, a judge (who judged Israel for forty years) and a priest - but he is nowhere called a prophet and, indeed, Scripture introduces the story of Samuel's prophetic initiation by saying outright words I have already cited: "In those days, the word of

God was exceedingly rare and prophetic vision not at all widespread."

Yet, rare though it was to hear *or* see God, Eli, ninety-eight years old and mostly blind, didn't need much to realize that it was God who was calling out to Samuel, a fact that not only eluded Samuel himself, but which he, Samuel, continued to resist until the proof was overwhelming and his rationalist defences simply caved in under the weight of experiential evidence too profound to be fobbed off with mere intellectual theorizing about the likelihood or reasonableness of having the experience he was actually having at that very moment.

Eli himself had a sorry fate, but his life of service and worship paid off in the end. And so our story finishes off with poor, ancient, blind Eli somehow able to perceive God's voice - or at least its distant echo - when it came to his disciple. Would any of us be satisfied to devote a century to worship in exchange for an echo? The older I get, the more reasonable it sounds ....

8. Kên Baqqodesh Ḥazitikhah

There are always two ways.
Judaism - the modern religion of the Jewish people - is the result of a careful blending of post-exilic efforts to recapture what those ancients considered to be the even *more* ancient spirituality of Israel long after the institutions that provided that antique faith with its frame and substance were either defunct entirely or else (dramatically or slightly) transformed by the same catalysts that still transform society in our own day: the alienation that derives from exile, the rage that results from political impotence, and the profound dismay that comes about as a function of sudden, unanticipated contact with ancillary civilizations no less sure of the legitimacy, power and authenticity of their own gods than one's own people were when they were supreme masters in their own house.

The fifteen or so decades between the arrival of Ezra the Scribe in Jerusalem at the beginning of the fourth century and the translation of the Torah into Greek sometime around the middle of the third century saw the production of the book we call Torah as an effort to transform the private spirituality of the Jerusalem priesthood into a public blend of ritual and dogma that could satisfy the spiritual yearnings of a people no longer willing simply to sponsor the religion of the priesthood by paying for it or showing up now and then in the course of the year to look at it.

As I have explained above, this same post-exilic Jewish world also produced another book, *Tehillim*, the Book of Psalms - a collection of old and new songs that reflected a different kind of ancient spirituality, that of the prophet rather than the priest. There's no question that many of the songs in the book were thought of as ancient even then - but the question is not so much how old any individual poem among the psalms is, but why the people who put together this *particular* hymnal found this *particular* gross of songs to be reasonable and proper hymns to include in their hymnal. Individual psalms may come from older, pre-exilic times, but the Psalter itself is a post-exilic work. Of that, there can be no serious doubt at all. And its compilers - if not necessarily the authors of every single one of its constituent poems - were the Levites of the post-exilic world who served in the Jerusalem Temple under the authority of the priests.

How did the groups that produced these two works view each other? It's hard to say, but, as I've already mentioned, the evidence suggests that there wasn't too much love lost between them. The Torah, for its part, stakes out its position in fairly bald terms as God is heard (or rather, overheard) to say that He has specifically taken the Levites (hithertofore just one among twelve different tribes) and given them over as sanctuary slaves (if such be the correct translation of the Hebrew *netunim*) to the priests. Given that kind of no-nonsense hostility, the Torah's famous story of the rebellion of Korach, which basically tells in detail how God had no choice but to execute those renegade Levites who dared challenge the authority of the Aaronide priesthood, makes perfect sense. (And the fact that eleven psalms were later attributed, perhaps slightly defiantly, to the "sons of Korach" only shows the circle closing even more tightly. Had the Levites expressed their spirituality through story rather than through song, the tale of Korach's rebellion would have presumably come out quite a bit differently!)

On the other hand, the Psalter refers to the priesthood only here and there, mostly either to *nod* to their suffering at the fall of Jerusalem, to *predict* (rather snidely, I think) that *they* will finally (or rather, probably) get to know God up close in messianic times and, possibly, to *damn* with the faintest of praise by noting that the priests had nice, well-oiled beards. Far more to the point, the themes of persecution and public ridicule are major themes in the Psalter, themes that recur over and over in almost countless passages and which are expressed, I think, in language redolent of the kind of despair that comes from rejection at the hands of people one wants to be able to trust and for whose acceptance one ardently wishes - but from whom one knows better than to expect anything more than grief and ridicule.

The hymns of the Psalter are the stuff of the neo-prophetic communion with God pursued by at least some groups within Levitical circles during the early Second Temple period. That's why they're they're in the Psalter in the first place, after all - because the Levitical editors of the book deemed these poems and not others to mirror their own intense spirituality. We can read them as great poetry, certainly, but we can also mine them for information about the search for experiential knowledge of God in what was perhaps the most formative period of Jewish spiritual history. There are always two ways, you see.

The sixty-third psalm is a good example and it is with this particular poem that we begin. The author is deep into the fantasy that his own spiritual search for sensual communion with God is made legitimate not merely (that is, after the fact) by the success he has experienced, but by the fact that his efforts were pioneered by no less unimpeachably legitimate a historical personality than David, King of Israel, himself.

The poet begins by imagining (himself as) David in the wilderness. (The poem begins with the words "A psalm of David when he was in the wilderness of Judah", but whether that superscription is part of the original poem or simply the first of many subsequent attempts to determine the specific incident in David's life that prompted its composition, I don't know.) At any rate, the commentators fill in the details, all of which seem right to me: that the specific scene being conjured up is the one in which David is in the Wilderness of Ziph fleeing from Saul as he tried to make his way to Kiryat Yearim, where the Ark of God was stored after the destruction of the sanctuary at Shiloh. Whether or not this was what the actual author of the poem had in mind as he wrote his psalm is ultimately irrelevant here, by the way. What I want to wonder about is how the Levites who actually *used* this psalm as part of their spiritual regimen of song understood it. And it's into that question, I think, that the traditional commentators can provide deep insight.

At any rate, the story of David in the Wilderness of Ziph is told twice in the Bible, once in the twenty-third and twenty-fourth chapters of the First Book of Samuel and then again in the twenty-sixth chapter. Some of the details are different, but the story itself is basically the same in both places and it seems likely both versions are simply different accounts of the same incident. Saul is king of Israel, but he has already been told by his mentor Samuel that God has rejected his claim to kingship and "given it to one worthier than he." And it isn't only the slow process by means of which the throne is to be taken from his house that has begun either: Saul's personal descent into madness has also commenced, crystallized for the latter-day reader in Saul's (not entirely unjustified) paranoia regarding David and his place in the royal scheme of things.

In both versions of the story, David stops being the pursued, hunted party and turns, somehow, into the pursuer.

The second story takes place precisely in the Wilderness of Ziph, but in the first version of the story, David has already passed through that particular desert and has entered the wilderness of Ein Gedi. (Ein Gedi is still there, by the way, and is one of Israel's most beautiful natural sites. A friend of mine once broke his ankle there.) Anyway, for some reason, David is in the back of a cave when Saul, hot in pursuit, stops in to relieve himself before continuing his search. Is David hiding? Or is he resting? Scripture is unclear, but the basic set-up is classic: David suddenly finds himself a few feet from the very man who is hunting him.

The picture in the cave is all the more piquant for being so delightfully vulgar. The king has turned around to face out towards the mouth of the cave as he squats over his make-shift privy hole, his long, royal robes pushed back behind him where they're less likely to get messed. David creeps up stealthily in the dark, the sound of his muffled footfalls presumably masked, one can only assume, either by the king's grunting or by the reverberating churning and gurgling of the royal bowels as they void, if not by both.

David sneaks up slowly, perhaps uncertain up until the last moment what his plan actually is. Should he murder the king? Saul certainly hasn't been making any bones about wanting to do away with David, having sent men to kill him more than once and even having called him a *ben mavvet* - a man marked for death - openly, a remark we can only assume would have reached David's ears one way or the other. From the back of the cave, David can hear the anxious breathing of his own men, loyal soldiers whose stage whispers behind their master egging him on to regicide are preserved in Scripture with neither censure, regret nor overt approval.

Slowly he approaches, his dagger in his hand. He lifts his hand, only to be visited by a sudden revelation: Saul is the anointed of God and his murder would thus be as much a kind of deicide by proxy as it would be *mere* treason. (That's the whole point of anointing monarchs in the first place, after all: to grant them the strange, but highly desirable, status of being God's chosen instruments of governance and thus attackable - not to mention murderable - only by those who hate God.) And so David has to decide: to act or not to act? To slay the king or to throw himself on the mercy of the king? To rely on his own experience of the divine (according to which he himself is to become king) or to rely on the popular perception of God's will (according to which Saul is the legitimate monarch to whom all fealty is due)?

Let's stop the story for a moment and flash forward to its second version, the one preserved a few chapters later in the same book. Here, we are back in the Wilderness of Ziph proper. Saul is pursuing David and hears that he is hiding out in a place called Givat Hahakhilah, so he heads over there with no less than three thousand men. In this version, Saul doesn't step into a cave to relieve himself, but simply lies down on the ground to sleep for the night. Scripture paints a deeply evocative picture with only a few words. It is the middle of the night. Saul is asleep in the middle of a circle of officers pledged to defend his life. The moon hangs overhead, its silvery light barely illuminating the desert landscape as the royal party slumbers on. David and his nephew Abishai ben Zeruiah sneak into the king's camp. The snoring of the king's men masks the almost imperceptible footfalls of the two interlopers, making of them little more than two shadows cast by white moonlight across a barren wilderness.

Slowly, they approach the sleeping king and, as they do, they can see the details of the setting that had been invisible only moments earlier. The king is lying on the ground, his sword jammed into the earth by his head. His loyal men are sleeping in a circle around him, their leader Abner easily recognizable in their midst. A water jar sits near the king's head as well, a useless clay sentinel pointlessly taking in the details that would have been apparent to Abner and his men had they not been slumbering away when they ought to have been guarding the king's life.

In this version of the story, it is Abishai who offers to kill Saul, promising to dispatch him with one single thrust of the king's own sword. The irony of executing the king with his own weapon is exquisite, but the implications of murdering the anointed one of God are too much for David, who settles for stealing the king's sword and water jug. Is it amazing that David could enter the leave the camp without being caught? The author of the Biblical story thought it unlikely too: he explains that it was no ordinary slumber that immobilized the king's men, but a *tardêmah* of God that had come over them.

The dark slumber of God - the *tardêmat hashem* of the Biblical text - is deeply evocative to the savvy reader, recalling both the celestial torpor with which God immobilized (and, one can only hope, anaesthetized) Adam as He made Eve of one of his ribs and also the sleep which God cast upon Abraham at the great ceremony that finally established the formal terms of their covenantal relationship, a sleep so deep that the Biblical text itself pauses to explain the term as being the equivalent of a "great, dark dread."

The ends of both stories are fairly upbeat. In the first one, David waits for the king to pull up his ermine britches (if that's what the kings of Israel wore under their greaves) and exit the cave, then calls out to him, using (a bit pathetically) the honorific title "Father". And then he produces a bit of fabric he cut from the royal cloak to prove that he, David, could have slain his king but didn't. Saul, unexpectedly, is touched by David's forbearance. He weeps openly, forgives David his destiny (despite its depressing implications for the House of Saul) and, in the somewhat laconic words of the Biblical text, "goes home."

The second story also ends on a note of reconciliation. David taunts Abner for having been such a useless bodyguard, but Saul hears David's voice and, moved by David's gesture of non-hostility, openly admits that he was wrong to pursue David, whom he (also a bit pathetically) now calls "my son." Again here, Saul concedes his destiny to David and the story ends on the same note as the previous one: with David and Saul, their peace made and their business with each other concluded, each going home. It's true that David takes advantage of the truce to flee to Philistia lest the king change his mind, but that's another story ....

I've gone on at some length, but only to set the stage for reading the words of the sixty-third psalm. The poet starts out, as I said above, by imagining David's mindset as he hides from Saul. He - David - is destined to be king of Israel, but he isn't exactly living the life of a prince - indeed, he is living the life of a vagabond, hiding out in the kind of dark, damp caves real kings use as latrines and wandering from place to place in the hope of finding a safe refuge from the mad king's fury.

In other words, the poet imagines his spiritual ancestor David in much the same position with respect to Saul that he himself is in with respect to God, his own King. The poet is a Levite, a temple functionary. The worship of God is his bread and butter, the stuff of his daily fare. Serving God, after all, is what he does all day both professionally *and* spiritually. If anyone should be enjoying his privileged position within the sacerdotal hierarchy of old Jerusalem, it should logically be he - and yet his soul is sad. He is no less one of God's chosen servants than David was God's anointed one ... but, at least at the moment, he can only perceive God from a distance, sensing His presence in a formal, rather than a truly intimate way. And he's not *only* worried about the fulfilment of his spiritual destiny either - he's worried about being attacked and beaten, possibly even killed, by powerful enemies entirely secure in their convictions regarding their own spiritual status and worth. Was the Levite a *ben mavvet* - a condemned man - in the sense Saul used the term of David? I don't think so and certainly hope not - but the kinship the poets whose songs fill our Psalter felt with David is certainly primarily with the fugitive rather than with the successful, established monarch into which David evolved years later.

His soul, the poet's soul, is thirsting for God the same way parched land thirsts for water. And it is not mere faith in God that he wishes to attain - for he is one of those Levites who has already experienced sensual, visual communion with God and wishes it again and again. *Kên baqqodesh ḥazitikhah* he writes, meaning that he has seen God in the sanctuary in the past and now wishes to see him again. His vocabulary is the vocabulary of prophecy: *ḥazitikhah* is a form of one of the two or three most basic classical Hebrew verbs denoting the visual experience of God.

Was the Levite the author of the psalm or was he simply using an older poem as a vehicle for the expression of his own spiritual longing? If he was its author, then was he writing his poem as a kind of spiritual confession or as a hymn intended to be chanted by other seeking to see God? It is obviously no longer possible to know the answer to such obscure questions, but the implications of the poet's remarks are clear: he has known God not merely as one of His loyal priests, but as one of the faithful who know Him intimately. No wonder this poem made it into the Psalter: it mirrors the aspirations of the latter-day Levitical seekers to real communion with a visible, communicative Deity almost perfectly. I can't prove it, but I think they were responsible for writing this poem, not merely for preserving it.

Later in his hymn, the poet writes that his soul cleaved unto God even as he felt himself being supported by an unseen divine force - in other words, he felt God allowing Himself to be cleaved unto by the poet's soul - thus indicating that He seeks His faithful by allowing Himself to be sought, not unlike (except in every way imaginable) the way Saul only *found* David once he allowed himself *to be found* by David.

At the end of his hymn, the poet turns to one of the favourite themes of the Book of Psalms as a whole: the suffering those who seek God must endure at the hands of those who scoff at their efforts. Who were these scoffers who made the poet's life so miserable? Were they obscure villains who hated the poet for specific reasons we can only guess at? Or were they priests who laughed at and scorned the efforts of the Levites to develop a new kind of post-exilic prophetism that would hold the concept of visual (or, at least, auditory) communion with God to be the ultimate goal of honest religious effort and spiritual endeavour? Or were they other Jerusalemites, people for whom the service of God was a tax owed, not an unbearable thirst left unquenched for as long as they were obliged by their own laziness and apathy to endure life without the palpable presence of God in their personal sensual ambits. At any rate, the poet doesn't mince any words, wishing aloud that his enemies all go straight to hell once their gutted bodies are fed to wild foxes.

And so, twenty-five centuries or so later, we take up the journey towards God. Our guidebook is no guidebook at all, merely a collection of oracles and poems collected into a larger work by an ancient anthologizer so that poetry inspired by the experience of seeing and hearing God might inspire others to seek still greater heights of sensual knowledge of the divine. The clues are few and far between, often couched in the most obscure language of symbol and metaphor. The author of the sixty-third psalm reveals many different facets of himself in his poem, but of his experience of gazing on God, he says only that it happened in the Qodesh, i.e. in the sanctum of the Jerusalem Temple. The Levites, whose hymns over and over identify the various courtyards and sanctuaries of the Temple as the ideal place in which to seek out the sensually perceptible presence of God, must have liked that. Did the Levites of the old Jerusalem Temple expect their book to be cherished by millions of people all over the world twenty-five centuries after their own day? It seems unlikely ... but the lessons their book bears to those who still seek God are as eternal as the book itself appears to be.

From this particular psalm, we learn that God may (or is it must?) be sought in a holy place. And what does tradition teach constitutes a holy place? When Moses approached the burning bush, God told him he was standing on holy ground. When Joshua approached the angelic captain of the Lord's host in a field near Jericho a generation later, he was told the same thing. It was not a temple in which either man was standing, and neither did either scene play itself out in a shrine of any sort, not even in one of the much maligned high places of Biblical antiquity. The holiness, then, of those places apparently derived solely from the fact that God was perceptible in them. Now our tradition is unequivocal on this point: that the omnipresent God is (almost of necessity) everywhere perceptible as well. Does that mean that any place in which God is sought is by definition a holy place? Whether that is so or not, I can't say with certainty - but the fact remains that it was in a holy place that the Levites gathered late at night to seek God ... to seek Him and to see Him and to hear His voice. Did they choose that place because it was already a holy place ... or did they choose it specifically so that its holiness - not its historic sanctity, but its ongoing aura of divine presence - could be maintained through their efforts to know God in that place? Or did they seek God's palpable presence in the Temple simply because that was where they lived and worked and where the priests (for all their haughtiness, not necessarily wrongly) insisted that the aspect of God terrestrials may know was especially, perhaps even solely, accessible? The answers to those questions, dear readers, is lost in the mists of history, but one clue remains for us to ponder as we wonder how to go about seeking the kind of intimacy with the divine realm to which our Levitical ancestors so passionately aspired. Kên baqqodesh ḥazitikhah, the poet wrote: "I (for one) saw You in the Holy Place." We can, therefore, begin no more logically than by seeking out a place of holiness in our world from which to set out towards a life in God. And how are we to know a holy place possessed of that kind of spiritual potential when we find one? That, at least, we can learn from the stories Scripture tells about Moses and Joshua: it is any place, any place at all.

9. *'Esbe'ah Behaqitz Temunatekhah*

The author of the poem we call the seventeenth psalm starts off a bit slowly, labelling his effort merely as a prayer of David and leaving it for his readers to guess what specific incident in David's life was inspiring him.

It's not an easy poem. And the author's archaizing style, intended to remind his readers (he no doubt hoped) of the Hebrew of David's day, only makes the water even muddier than it would otherwise be. Still, the basic outline of the poet's religious world view is apparent and, for me, highly relevant. And I think I can see why such a way of looking at the world would have appealed to people trying to know God in a visceral, physical way.

Like the author of the sixty-third psalm - and like the authors of dozens of other poems in the Psalter - this poet too feels persecuted and hard done by. When he writes that his vindication will come from God, there's no problem catching his depressed drift: from *God* his absolution might (possibly, maybe even certainly) come, but not from frail, stupid, biased, bigoted human beings. When he calls on God to guard him "like the apple of His eye" from his mortal enemies - nameless scoundrels who are encroaching from every direction - there's no easy way, even for us jaded modern types, to dismiss his poetry as nothing more profound than the disheartened snivelling of a professional whiner. And when he switches, just for a brief moment, from the plural to the singular to describe his nemesis as "a lion eager for prey lying in hidden ambush" and calls upon God to rise up and strike the scoundrel down, there's no logical reason to interpret (and thereby to dismiss) his plaint as a generalized lament about the relative strength of goodness and evil in the world. The poet was a real human being who had a real enemy, one who loathed him and belittled him and who mocked him, as my favourite English teacher used to say, on a variety of levels.

About the poet's anonymous enemy, I don't have much information to offer. But there's quite a bit I can say about the psalmist himself. For one thing, he was a person who longed for God to speak to him directly. Indeed, I think the sixth verse of his poem could accurately be translated to yield the idea that God will speak to him *precisely* because he has called on God in the *precisely* right way to catch His ear and, presumably, to awaken within Him the desire to speak. But the poet doesn't only want to hear God's voice, he wants to see God as well. And he doesn't mind saying so.

The last verse of his poem is as confident as it is precise. *'Ani betzedeq 'ehezeh panekhah*, he writes, *'esbe'ah behaqitz temunatekhah*. I give the words in Hebrew first because practically each one is laden with enough layers of evocative meaning to make it almost impossible to present it in English translation with anything but the palest, most ordinary accuracy.

To begin with the end, the poet is clear about what he wants: not merely to see God in some sort of dream vision, but to see Him in a waking state in the manner of the great pre-exilic prophets. Now, a few dozen centuries later, that might sound a bit banal. But in the context of the world in which the author lived, those were - to put it mildly - fighting words. And the punch they packed can only be gauged in terms of the degree to which they conflict with other received texts that present us with their own claim to unimpeachable authority. Indeed, the various instances of prophetic communion with God that were written up and preserved in the Bible are more or less *all* described precisely as waking visions. Yet, when the (priestly) Torah itself turns to the subject of such intimate experiences of the divine, it could not be clearer in its assertive, unambiguous insistence that Moses alone enjoyed that kind of familiarity with God. Moses, but no other prophet. Ever.

Perhaps we should look at that passage before we go on. In the twelfth chapter of the Book of Numbers, Scripture tells a brief story about the discomfort Aaron and Miriam felt with their brother Moses' status as divine confidant extraordinaire. The precise details of their complaint and the exceptional response it elicits are not that important in this context, but the words Scripture offers as God's response to their impudence are. It's the *other* prophets, the Torah insists, who see God in dreams and visions - but Moses is different.

God speaks to him "mouth to mouth", a phrase parallel both to the remark in Moses' obituary to the effect that God spoke to him "face to face" and to the notice elsewhere in Scripture to the effect that God spoke to Moses "as one man speaks with another."

But it's not only how he *hears* that the Torah insists distinguishes Moses from the other prophets - it's specifically how he *sees* as well. It seems that they - the other prophets - do indeed see God in their dreams. Now this is a bit of a stunning anachronism in the text - are we really supposed to imagine that enough time has passed between the episodes related in the eleventh and twelfth chapters of the book to allow the Torah to make generalized statements about the kind of prophetic vision the newly invested prophet-elders of Israel are wont to have? - but the more important point here is the assertion that Moses is unique. *Temunat hashem yabit*, the text asserts: Moses sees the *temunah* of God, precisely the aspect of God the psalmist specifically wants to see, while they, the other (and lesser) prophets, see something else, something less precise and, by extension, less transcendant. And what's more, when Moses sees this kind of divine image, he sees it while he's awake rather than being asleep or in some sort of mystic trance, which is *precisely* how the poet himself intends to experience God as well.

So what is this *temunah*? In modern Hebrew, the word has come to mean simply "picture", which is what it appears to mean in the Ten Commandments when the faithful Israelite is forbidden to fashion an image, presumably a fetish of some sort, of any creature that flies in the air or lives in the sea or on the land. But can that be what the term means when we read that Moses was superior to the other prophets because he alone merited seeing the divine *temunah*, presumably something better (that is, more real *and* more intimate) than the kind of image the others were able to see in their dreams?

There's an interesting passage in the Torah that's probably highly relevant in this regard - the semi-famous line in which Moses reminds the people that Israel's experience at Sinai was one of (mere) junior-grade prophecy on a national scale: "God spoke to you from within the fire," he admits, adding "but you *only* heard the sound of spoken words." Those are my italics, not Moses', but the point he's making couldn't be clearer and then, just in case it needed to be, he returns to the topic a few lines later to make his point even more plainly: "You didn't perceive any *temunah*," he continues, apparently forgetting for the moment that his audience consisted pretty much solely of the *children* of the people who stood at Sinai, "just sound ...."

So we're left with the conclusion that, at least as far as our priestly Torah is concerned, there are three basic levels of prophecy: there's the mass experience the people had at Sinai during which they saw nothing at all of the divine image and were (or rather, had to be) content with hearing God's voice. Then, on a slightly more transcendant level, there are the prophets other than Moses who see *something* - something, but not the divine *temunah*. And then, of course, there's Moses himself, the only utterly transcendant prophet, who did indeed merit the experience of seeing God, *not* in visions or dreams, but in a waking experience in which he was able to perceive the actual divine image. (And even in Moses' case, it was an acquired taste - in its account of Moses' first up-close encounter with the divine at the burning bush, Scripture makes a point of insisting that he immediately covered his face once he realized what was happening "for he was afraid to look at God.")

Other passages in Torah, for example the famous aside that "no human being can see God and survive the experience," seem to buttress this general understanding of how people may perceive God. But this priestly view of things was apparently as foreign - and irrelevant - to the pre-exilic prophets as it was to their Levitical followers later on. *They* saw God and they *all* lived to tell the tale. What's more, they seem to have cultivated the experience with relish and enthusiasm - and without the slightest trace of suicidal mania. And what the author of the seventeenth psalm wants is *precisely* to experience the *temunah* of God in a waking, conscious state. To perceive God (if I may misquote Scripture slightly) "as one person might stand before another." To know God *precisely* as the Torah insists only Moses ever could. To survive *precisely* that experience of the divine that the Torah says unequivocally none but Moses could ever live through.

And he doesn't just want to taste this experience once or twice either. The verb he uses - *'esbe'ah* - implies that he wants to *gorge* himself on it, to experience it to complete (perhaps even excessive) satisfaction. (Another Biblical text uses the same verb to describe the way someone might cram so much honey into himself that he would actually have to puke *some* of it out before he could ever manage to digest *any* of it.) It's true that classical Hebrew also uses the term in a variety of less gross passages to denote simply satiety, but I think that the poet is using the term in its coarser sense here, just as he uses it elsewhere in this same poem to refer not simply to having *enough* wealth for one's own needs, but to having enough to leave behind as a bequest to one's children, which is to say: having more than enough.

The verb in the first half of his verse is also loaded. *'Ehezeh*, he says - shall *behold* the face of God. This verb too has its own deeply evocative connotative meaning in the history of Israelite prophecy. I've already mentioned above that the author of the Books of Samuel makes a special point of noting that the original Hebrew name for the ecstatic prophets of Israel was *hozim* - seers (or rather, see-ers), individuals who were so called (I assume) because they *beheld* God. Even the Torah, with its essentially negative view of prophecy, uses the term in its account of the great covenantal meal the elders held on the slopes of Sinai to mean precisely what it apparently did mean. *Vayehezu 'et ha'elohim*, the Torah says: the elders *beheld* God. (It's true that the Torah does seek to defuse the shock value of *that* remark by prefacing it with the note that in this exceptional instance - and, presumably, in this exceptional instance alone - God refrained from killing them for having done so. But that kind of backtracking-before-the-fact is just another example of the typical priestly knee-jerk reaction even to the intimation that anyone but Moses could *ever* have beheld the divine *temunah*.)

So if we put all that together, we can indeed interpret the last verse of the seventeenth psalm as an ancient poet's self-assurance that *despite* the insults and attacks of his enemies and *despite* the hostility of the priestly overlords and their anti-prophetic Torah and *despite* the almost terrifying hubris inherent even in the idea (let alone the actual practice) of seeking to see God–despite it all, "I am justified to seek Your face and, indeed, I shall gorge myself on the waking, conscious experience of Your *temunah*."

As I noted above, the poet approaches us behind the mask of David, the ancient prophet-king of Israel whose inestimably great cachet was apparently deemed sufficient to justify the psalmists' efforts to gaze at the godhead. But of which particular event in David's life was he thinking? In other words, what *specific* event does the poet imagine led the king to write this *specific* poem?

Radak, whose commentary to the psalms is among the most psychologically and theologically astute of them all, writes that it was in the aftermath of the incident involving Uriah the Hittite (and his lovely wife, Bathsheba) that David wrote this particular psalm.

The story is one of the Bible's best known, but perhaps I should retell it briefly just in case you've repressed (or forgotten or never knew) some of the details. It starts off with David having a smoke (or something) on the roof of his palace late one afternoon. He's strolling around and suddenly he sees a beautiful woman bathing on her own (slightly lower) roof. David takes great interest, makes the appropriate inquiries and learns that she is none other than Bathsheba, wife of Uriah the Hittite, one of David's soldiers.

Anyway, one thing leads to another and before you know it - the Biblical storyteller delicately covers this part of the story in half of one sentence - she's pregnant. David is not amused. (Neither, we may assume, is Bathsheba, but she doesn't say much in the story. In fact, she doesn't say anything at all unless you want to count sending a two-word note ("I'm pregnant!") as saying something. Of course, the story is about him, not her ... but still, you'd have thought the storyteller would at least give her something to do aside from getting pregnant, letting David know and (presumably) making her peace with what comes next. But he didn't.)

At any rate, what does come next is that David has to act quickly to cover up his misdeed. Of course, there wouldn't be that much to cover up if Uriah were living at home and sleeping with his wife - she could always claim that the child was her husband's even if he did somehow inherit David's red hair - but Uriah is simply too decent a fellow - this is Biblical irony at its best - to take pleasure in his own bed while his fellow soldiers are bivouacking it in the field even if he *is* legitimately on leave at home. So David goes to plan B: he sends word to General Joab and gets Uriah put in the front lines when he returns, whereupon he is duly killed during the next skirmish with the Ammonites. End of problem.

Not exactly. David moves Bathsheba into the palace about eight seconds after her formal period of mourning ends. Scripture doesn't say precisely how long *that* was, but we can presume Bathsheba was installed in the seraglio in plenty of time for no one to find it unreasonable for David to acknowledge her unborn child as his own.

Now the prophet Nathan gets involved. God makes the situation clear to the prophet, who comes to David with a parable about a rich man who steals a poor man's lamb to roast for lunch one day when a friend drops in unexpectedly. Nathan lays it on a bit thick -

the best part is when he says the lamb was such a beloved member of the poor man's family that it was almost a daughter to him - but David still misses the point, taking Nathan's story for an account of a real incident and deciding on the spot that the rich man should be put death *and* (if that's not enough) fined four times the cost of a replacement lamb as a (presumably posthumous) punishment for his larcenous greed. Nathan, who had presumably hoped for just that response, now summons up his courage and faces the king. *Atah ha'ish*, he says - "You are that man!" - packing more righteous indignation into two words than most authors can in two chapters.

What follows are only just desserts: since David was prepared to murder for the sake of his desire for another man's wife, so shall he have to endure the ignominy of knowing that another man shall sleep with some of his own wives. And not only that, but the child with whom Bathsheba is pregnant shall die.

Both predictions come true - with the added ironic twist that it is none other than David's own son, Absalom, who ends up sleeping with ten of his father's concubines - but David doesn't need to wait to see either fulfilled. "I have sinned before God," he declares openly and guilelessly. And the prophet wastes no time in delivering the message of divine absolution David so intently desired. "God has removed your sin," he declares confidently, adding that David shall not die, even if the son to be born unto him must.

From the Jewish perspective, this (and neither the death of Uriah *nor* the child's death) is the centre of the story and its high point: the moment of repentance so pure and real that it alone serves to avert the divine decree - even though the child's life must still be forfeit. And this is the moment to which the commentators assign the composition of the seventeenth psalm. We can quibble about whether the poem was written by David himself or by a late poet writing *as* David, but the more essential point is the poet's cry for vindication as he contemplates the bitter aftermath of his sin ... and his no less authentic assertion, all the more moving given its awful context, that, justified, he shall yet behold the face of God and not *only* see it in the normal prophetic way, but actually stuff himself with the experiential knowledge of God to the point of satiety (and then some).

The poet knows he has sinned, as all terrestrials must. But he has done his best to achieve a state of total repentance and he wishes to be rewarded for *those* efforts in a way as profoundly meaningful as the appropriate punishment for his misdeeds would have been severe. I imagine him figuring that he can't possible have sinned as grievously as David, then asking himself why his reward then should be any less great. It's not such a bad question ....

No one who yearns to know God cannot pause, at least occasionally, to wonder about the inherent blasphemy in the whole enterprise of any human being seeking to gaze on the godhead in the first place. After all, Scripture does say fairly unequivocally that no human may see God and survive the experience. And if the accounts of the prophets seem to belie that assertion, then that surely only leaves us on the horns of a difficult dilemma, not resting comfortably in the afterglow of its resolution!

The seventeenth psalm, especially if Radak was right about the incident in David's life that inspired it, offers a second clue, dear readers. There is regret in this world and there's also remorse. But to overwhelm the sense of crippling, blasphemous absurdity that continually threatens to destabilize any thinking individual's quest for God, neither will suffice. To stand in the presence of God, one must first learn how to return unto God in complete repentance, that state of transcendental contrition that transfigures the individual who experiences it and makes that person, like Saul at Givat Ha'elohim, into a different person than he or she was a moment earlier.

Like all truly religious experiences, repentance cannot be sought in the rules of complex rituals and neither can it be prepared for or induced through the singing of hymns or the study of sacred texts. It is, therefore, something elusive and very difficult to attain ... but it's also the natural condition of the human heart that longs for God with a purity of purpose unsullied by laziness, apathy or greed, the absolutely requisite state that one must attain prior to seeking to know God sensually and passionately. And so we have it put plainly: to see God, one must first dare to look honestly and openly at oneself ....

10. 'Aḥat Sha'alti

> ... a treasure of King David
> committed to my trust - the
> final hope of the sad Jews ...
> Racine

Like the other poets we've been looking at, the author of the twenty-seventh psalm was not a happy camper. Evil men assailed him. Villains tried to devour his flesh. (I assume that's a metaphor.) Armies besieged him. He lived in an ongoing state of war with unnamed (but presumably not unknown) enemies. He experienced days he could only think to characterize as evil. He was denounced in court by false witnesses whose testimony inspired violence against him. He was under constant surveillance ....

This poet is also like the others in that he too writes behind the mask of David, preferring to temper the shocking reality of his personal situation by projecting it onto the distant past. The commentators vie with each other to find the precise point in David's life with which the author of the twenty-seventh psalm was so deeply identified.

For Sforno, that point wasn't a single event at all, but rather the long, protracted period of his flight from the wrath of Saul. Confused by the internal conflict between (on the one hand) the natural desire of any faithful courtier to serve his king and (on the other) his own sense of self-preservation, David turned to poetry to express both his outrage at the impossibility of his situation *and* his faith in the ultimate ability of God to resolve his dilemma reasonably.

For the Meiri, the psalm is just a general policy statement of David's in which the young king wished to give formal voice to - and thus, perhaps, to justify - the practice of seeking victory over his enemies not for the sake of honour or pleasure, but simply because living in peace was the sole way of which the king knew to free himself from the burdens of monarchy and governance sufficiently and long enough for him to be able to turn his attention fully to the worship of God.

For Ibn Ezra, the twenty-seventh psalm (like the 110th) is a prayer of the elderly David. Some time after the aborted rebellion of a certain Sheba ben Bichri against David was put down, Ibn Ezra suggests, things started to go less well for the elderly king. He bowed to the macabre demand of the residents of the city of Gibeon that two of Saul's sons and five of his grandsons be turned over to them for execution. (They were subsequently decapitated and their heads displayed on the side of a local mountain.) He became weary and was almost killed by Ishbibenob, one of the few remaining Philistine giants. (Luckily, David's life was saved by his nephew Abishai ben Zeruiah, who attacked the giant and killed him.)

But David's men had seen enough. "You shall not go into battle with us any longer," they said, politely (but not *too* politely) insisting that they were being motivated by concern for the security of the dynasty rather than by any worries they might have been having about their own safety if they were to be led into battle by a doddering senescent. And it was in the context of this moment - of humiliation, of rejection, of forced retirement and of unwanted, probably unexpected, insight into his own mortality - that Ibn Ezra imagines David retiring to his tent to pen the two poems later included in the Psalter as the 27th and 110th psalms.

Rashi's setting for the composition of the twenty-seventh psalm is even more elaborately far-fetched. David, Rashi knows, was a seer possessed of the intense insight into the future history of his people typical of all true prophets. And so, Rashi suggests, it came to pass one day that David had a vision of the future, of an event that would take place in the lifetime of his great-great-great-great-great-great grandson, King Joash of Judah. It's a long, shocking story, but it's a good one too and I tell it, therefore, with both relish and regret.

Unfortunately, it's also fairly complicated. The basic idea has to do with the fact that when Jehu ben Jehoshafat ben Nimshi assassinated King Joram of Israel (slightly at the behest of the prophet Elisha, who had secretly sent one of his disciples to anoint him - Jehu - as king), he also killed King Ahaziah of Judah for good measure.

What exactly Ahaziah was doing in the northern kingdom instead of ruling Judah safely from his palace in Jerusalem is another story, but the basic idea is that he was killed and his mother, the wicked Athaliah - the Lady Macbeth of Biblical antiquity - responded to her son's death in the style of her own murderous mother, Queen Jezebel of Israel, and promptly had all her grandsons murdered lest any of them grow up to challenge her personal claim (as Queen Mother) to the throne.

Unfortunately (for Athaliah), Ahaziah had a half-sister named Jehosheba who secretly took the king's infant son and hid him in the Temple for seven years. (This was possibly facilitated by the fact that Jehosheba was married to the High Priest Jehoiada.) Scripture doesn't say precisely where in the Temple she hid the little prince - this was the future King Joash - but legend has it that it was in the attic chamber directly over the Holy of Holies that he was kept ... and it was this particular idea of the baby growing to age seven (when he was finally crowned and his grandmother assassinated) in the most sacred space imaginable that inspired the prophetic David to pen the twenty-seventh psalm. Indeed, Rashi indicates that the words "He grants me shelter in his pavilion (Hebrew: *sukkah*) on a day of evil" refer specifically to the prince's experience of being hidden in the Temple for all those long years of Athaliah's evil reign.

Perhaps we can combine these last two approaches to the poem. David is a tired old man. He's suffered the indignity of being gently retired by his own troops. (Gently, but firmly: "You shall not go into battle ..." not "How would you feel, O Illustrious Sire, about staying back on the sidelines just this once while we go forth to risk our own worthless lives on your regal behalf ...?") The conqueror of the legendary Goliath of Gath has already suffered the ignominy of barely escaping with his life when he stoops to take on some Philistine nobody with the ridiculous name of Ishbibenob. He can practically *feel* the pity his men are developing for their aging monarch as they watch him decline ....

And then, perhaps precisely in the wake of being told to stay back while his men sally forth to take on the Philistine hordes, David has a vision. He looks into the future and sees the very Temple in Jerusalem he himself has been forbidden (by God!) to build. And what does he see? He sees what is to become of the dynasty his men are so worried about preserving. He sees the bodies of Ahaziah's children being pitched into unmarked graves. He sees Athaliah triumphantly proclaiming herself Queen of Israel before she's even had the time to wash the incriminatory blood of her own grandchildren off her villainous feet. And he sees tiny Prince Joash hidden in the secret chamber Solomon is going to build (by divine inspiration, no doubt) just over the Holy of Holies - the single spot that even a jezebel like Athaliah might (might!) think twice about desecrating.

Suddenly, David is overcome with a desire than cannot be fulfilled. He wants only one thing - and so he writes in the twenty-seventh psalm, "One thing do I ask of the Lord, only one thing do I seek" - and that one thing is to dwell in the House of God for however many days the king has left and to gaze there on the beauty of God and to tarry (perhaps after having experienced this intense, visual communion with the divine realm) for as long as he wished in the specific part of the Jerusalem sanctuary in which such instances of neo-prophetic communion apparently occurred. Okay, that's three things - but the idea is clear enough even if the king's arithmetic is a bit off. He wants to seek refuge in the presence of God, in the presence of the same God Who (he intuits) is going to protect the baby Joash for seven long years. He wants to move beyond the humiliation of his personal situation and transcend the world *and* its miseries by seeking communion with God. But the poet doesn't imagine David merely wishing to have his faith in God confirmed or even strengthened. He wishes to gaze *with his own tired eyes* on the beauty of the divine form. And he wishes to have that image of inexpressible beauty before his eyes not once or twice or even whenever he wishes to conjure it up - he wants it permanently, as a kind of filter through which he intends to view the rest of the world. He wishes to be a prophet not in the vague sense or in the theoretical sense, but in the ultimate sense. He wishes to see God.

The words the poet puts in David's mouth are drawn from the language of prophecy. When he says that he longs to gaze on God, the word for gaze is the same Hebrew word used of the elders at Sinai, regarding whom it is written in the priestly Torah that "they gazed on God." When he refers to the beauty of God, he uses the Hebrew word used in Israel's most vividly erotic poetry to describe the exquisite beauty of the Shulamith. When he talks of tarrying in the temple sanctuary, the word the prophet uses is the word Jeremiah later would use to condemn that very temple to destruction in one of his most famous diatribes against the corruption both of worshipper and priest in his day.

It's that image of David alone, lonely, rejected and abandoned that inspired the poet who apparently saw his own life reflected in the situation of the ancient king. Mocked by others, the poet seeks refuge in precisely the same thought that he imagines consoled David a half dozen centuries earlier: the thought that the experience of visual, sensual, ongoing prophetic communion with God is not merely its *own* reward in the theoretical sense, but also more than ample compensation for whatever unhappiness a life devoted to the cultivation of that experience might bring in its (slightly exclusionist) wake. And so the poem came into the Psalter. Those whose spirituality the poet's words endorsed had their own enemies to contend with - priests, less mystically-oriented Levites, the *hoi polloi* of old Jerusalem, perhaps even by their own parents ("For even though my father and mother have abandoned me, God Himself has gathered me unto Him") - and sought their solace in hymns like this one. Whether a Levite actually wrote these words or if they were bequeathed to the singers of the Second Temple by an earlier poet is irrelevant: what counts is that they spoke directly to the heart of the matter, to the situation in which the seekers of visual and auditory communion with God found themselves as they moved forward towards God in the context of the real world.

The search for the love of God is destined (if not quite guaranteed) to be fraught with difficulty and unhappiness. Devotion to cultivating (not mere belief in God, but) the actual experience of sensual perception of the divine will, more often than not, win the scorn of the less spiritually adept. (And, given the fact that no world could possibly be less supportive of spiritual enterprise than our own, the situation for moderns is only that much worse.) When another poet devoted to the search for mystic communion with God wrote that the Almighty is especially close to the broken-hearted, it seems likely that he was writing both from the heart and also about his own heart. And so we have our third clue: the success an individual will have in seeking to know God will vary inversely with the degree to which that person requires the encouragement and support of other people. Others can sell you the tickets and help you pack. Others can issue you your passport and drive you to the pier. But, at the end of the day, this is a journey you must make alone. Alone doesn't always (or necessarily) mean lonely. But it does always means alone. By yourself. With God once you find Him, but until then....unalterably, undeniably, unyieldingly alone.

11. *Yêshvu Yesharim 'Et Panekhah*

The author of the 140th psalm had a lot in common with the poets we've already discussed. (Don't forget that it's entirely possible that some, maybe even many, of these psalms were actually written by the same people. But in the absence of any real proof to the contrary, I'm going to write about their authors as though they were all separate people. Of course, that's also a conjecture with no real substance behind it ....)

At any rate, this guy is even less happy than the author of the twenty-seventh psalm. He too knows that there are lawless, wicked people out to get him. Is he speaking poetically when he writes about wicked laying out ropes and snares to capture him as he walks down the street - or is he reporting on some actual attempt to abduct him? It's hard to say, but he certainly sounds as though he means it, especially when he prays that his enemies be pitched into pits so deep they'll never climb out and then (presumably for good measure) covered with burning coals. (Why anyone would be that exercised against a poet is hard to say. Maybe they found his kind of spirituality threatening. Or maybe they found it irritating to have their own experiences of the divine tacitly denigrated by the intimacy claimed by those whose idea of knowing God was seeing Him and hearing Him and feeling His presence in their lives in a visceral, sensual, tactile way. Facing the same kind of unspoken insult to my own spirituality, I don't think I'd resort to violence. But I'd certainly find the situation intensely unpleasant.)

These miscreants aren't just generic gangsters who committed generic, vaguely defined crimes, either: their specialty was slander and libelous denunciation and we can only assume that the author was the subject of their calumny. They seem to have been eloquent ("They sharpen their tongues like serpents"), venomous ("Spiders' poison is dripping from their lips") and deliberate ("Their hearts are full of evil schemes / they plot war all day long.") And what, precisely, was it that they said about this particular person? That, the poet leaves out, but the commentators leave us a few choice observations that can be mined for some extra clues.

Ibn Ezra imagines that the poet is (or perhaps, is thinking of himself as) the young David fleeing for his life from the mad Saul and cursing (presumably in advance) those who might even think of denouncing him to the king, let alone those who might actually dare trap him with ropes and haul him into the royal court. Radak and the Meiri have the same idea, narrowing it down to the incidents with the Ziphites and with Doeg. I've already written about the Ziphites in connection with sixty-third psalm, but who was this Doeg? And what kind of slander was it he perpetrated against the young David?

It's a depressing story. Soon after Jonathan, Saul's son (and David's beloved friend) confirms that his father really is out to kill David, it becomes necessary (or at least prudent) for David to flee and the first town he comes to is a place called Nob - one of the places in which the Ark of the Covenant was kept after Shiloh was destroyed but before David moved it (eventually) to Jerusalem - where the shrine is presided over by a priest named Ahimelech. At first Ahimelech is a bit suspicious, but he calms down once David gives him some savvy answers and even lets David take some consecrated bread after he's assured that the men who are going to eat it - David's men whom he's on his way to meet up with - haven't had sex recently enough for it to be an issue. (Why that mattered in the first place is a different question - Ahimelech doesn't say and I won't either.)

Anyway, David takes the bread, then asks if Ahimelech doesn't have some sort of dagger or sword he might also take along with him. As it happens, not only does Ahimelech have a sword on hand, but it's none other than the sword of Goliath, the Philistine giant that David himself slew years earlier. It's wrapped up in some fabric and stored behind the ephod (whatever that was) and David is delighted to take it. "It's the best sword!" David enthuses as he unwraps it and moves on to visit King Achish of Gath.

The whole incident would hardly have been worth recording except for the fact that Ahimelech and David weren't quite as alone as they (or rather, Ahimelech - see below) thought they were.

Lurking in the shadows somewhere, it turns out, was one Doeg of Edom, Saul's chief shepherd (if that's what the slightly mysterious Hebrew title *'abir haro'im* really means.) Now it's true that Scripture is irritatingly (I suppose I should say tantalizingly) vague about the reasons for which Doeg was hanging around Nob on that particular day. Rashi follows the classical rabbis and writes that he had just dropped in to learn a bit of Torah in the shadow of the divine Tabernacle, presumably an auspicious place to study, when David happened by. Radak suggests that he must have come around with some friends to offer some sacrifices and then hung around after the rest went home either to say his prayers or to offer up some extra animals. The Rid writes that he really hadn't intended to be there at all - he had simply been caught there when the sun went down on Friday evening and had therefore been obligated to spend his Sabbath at Nob and was *still* there when David arrived on Saturday evening just after sundown. (Why an Edomite would feel obliged to refrain from travelling on the Jewish Sabbath is left unexplained in the Biblical text. Maybe he was a convert!) They're all reasonable answers, more or less, but the important point isn't *why* Doeg was in Nob in the first place, but *that* he was close enough by to take in the whole scene that played itself out between David and Ahimelech.

The next day, David moves on to his next hiding place and Doeg (pronounced in Hebrew in two syllables with the accent on the second so it rhymes with "poached egg") goes back to Saul or his sheep or whatever.

By this time, Saul has sunk into a state of truly demented paranoia. He's mean and he's angry and he's half mad anyway ... and this is the precise moment that Doeg steps out of the shadows and mentions that he happened to see Ahimelech of Nob giving David provisions *and* Goliath's sword. To put it mildly, Saul is not amused. He sends for Ahimelech and all the other priests, gives them a fair chance to confirm or deny Doeg's story and listens politely as Ahimelech first confirms the story and then sets to defending his actions. Excuses, the king isn't interested in hearing. He orders them all executed and then, when none of the king's personal servants is willing to strike down priests of God, he orders Doeg to do the job himself. Scripture doesn't record precisely what Doeg's reply to *that* was - or even if he *had* a specific reaction - but just notes that he, Doeg, had no qualms about killing Ahimelech and the other eighty-four priests of Nob. Then, for good measure, he goes on to dispatch all the other inhabitants of Nob as well: "men, women, children, infants, oxen, asses and sheep - all to the sword."

Later on, David admits to the single one of Ahimelech's sons to escape with his life that he actually *had* known that Doeg was there that day when he took the bread and the sword from Nob and that he also knew, or ought to have known, that a man like Doeg would go straight to Saul with such a juicy piece of scandalous information. Because he ought to have seen the implications of Doeg's presence, David accepts ultimate responsibility for the priests' deaths, but that is as much too little as it is much too late.

Anyway, that's the story of the talebearing Doeg and the awful carnage that his tattling brought in its wake. And that is the moment in David's life that both Radak and the Meiri think must have inspired the impassioned tirade against gossip and slander that is the 140th psalm.

Without knowing the particulars of his life, it's hard to say if the author was justified in seeing those who were slandering him as latter-day Doegs who wouldn't shrink from lifting their hands to murder servants of God - the Psalter specifically uses the title "servants of God" elsewhere to refer to the Levites on nighttime watch duty in the Temple - whom they found wanting or presumptuous in some unbearable way. But there's a certain urgency in the 140th psalm that suggests, especially (I think) in the Hebrew, that its author truly feared for his life. Or that's at least how I read it. Was that a realistic fear? It's hard to say, but it seems hard to imagine otherwise given the intensity of emotion packed into the poem's fourteen short verses.

And then, the punch line. After he calls down the most serious imprecations on the heads of his enemies, after he denounces them for their slanderous, murderous calumny against him, after he stops just short of accusing them of attempted murder...after all that, the poet finishes with the pious assertion that he *knows* that God will always champion the cause of the poor and the needy - probably both internal names for the group of mystic seekers of God to which the poet belonged - and that the upright shall live out their lives in the presence of God's face.

It's a fairly obscure line. Is the idea that the upright - perhaps yet another name for this particular group of Levitical mystics - were seeking to attain a state in which the sensually perceptible image of God's face was to be so permanently available to them that they could claim reasonably to be dwelling in its presence rather than merely dropping in to experience it, even intensely, from time to time? Or is the idea that the experience of knowing God and of gazing on the divine face was so profound and so moving so as to make all the suffering that belonging to the group of the upright brought in its wake worth (even perhaps well worth) the effort?

The bottom line is that the poet has a refuge from the world in the single aspect of his life and all its suffering that negates the pain, justifies the suffering and makes everything worthwhile. It isn't faith in God *per se* that makes the difference and neither is it the satisfaction that comes from following the rules of Torah really, really carefully. For the author of the 140th psalm, the only real way to justify a life spent scurrying from pillar to post in search of a place to escape from libel and calumny is to seek comfort and solace in the experience of seeing the face of God. And not merely in seeing it in the context of intense religious fervour, but actually living with it, dwelling *in* it, seeing it superimposed on the landscape of life as though God were some sort of omnipotent scrim separating the upright from the world and protecting them from it at the same time it *reveals* the world to them and grants them access to it.

The greatest impediments to attaining an ongoing experience of the sensually perceptible, empirically existent God in our lives are arrogance, self-puffery, and unwarranted pride in our own status in the world in which we live. The poet has no friends outside his tiny group of fellow travellers. Just to the contrary, he's surrounded - all day long, constantly - by wicked people hell-bent on his destruction. He seeks to dwell with God, therefore, at least partially because he fears to dwell with human beings. And so we come to our next clue. At a certain point, every adult learns that love - true, mature, abiding love - is less of a game than a long, lonely journey that can only be undertaken by an individual when he or she is ready and able to move slowly towards another—with all the vulnerability, self-knowledge and openness of emotion that such a move inevitably entails. The poet is intimating that the same is true of the journey towards God.

The world is hostile to most spiritual effort. Those who wait for the approbation or - even more absurdly - for the encouragement of the world as they grope their way towards God are doomed to spend their lives waiting for something that won't ever come. The key is to abandon the happy Sunday School image of a world of mutually supportive seekers of God helping one another and sustaining one another ... and to start interiorizing the poet's image of a hostile world of naysayers and hypocrites lying in wait along a dark road in the hope of ensnaring those who would journey to God and bringing them back into this world by addicting them to the awful conviction that God may be placated through worship, but never really encountered.

    The search, therefore, is not only lonely, but must also entail a certain degree of renunciation. Judaism is not an ascetic religion. We've never preached the spiritual value of poverty or suffering or celibacy. No, just to the contrary, our faith teaches us to marry, to raise children, to serve God by feasting on His festivals and Sabbaths ... but all that joy cannot obscure another truth: that the journey to God cannot be taken at the same time one is campaigning for the admiration of the world ....

12. *Yoshêv Hakkeruvim Hofi'ah*

The picture the Chronicler paints of David is a complex portrait of a man who plays many important roles and who sits at the top of a dozen different pyramids, each with a different set of underlings functioning as its living base. Thus David the General is provided by Scripture with a military hierarchy of generals and officers of various sorts. And David the King is provided with a parallel hierarchy of ministers and chamberlains to help him rule. In the same way, David the Prophet is provided with a hierarchy of prophets who serve him and under him. Of these, the three prophets-in-chief are Asaph, Heman and Jeduthun. I've already introduced these fellows, but since I'm about to discuss the eightieth psalm, which is attributed specifically to Asaph, perhaps I should reacquaint my readers with him just briefly.

It won't take long to say what we know because we don't know much. We know that his father's name was Berekhiah and that his family - he had four sons: Zakur, Joseph, Nathaniel and Asarelah belonged to the clan of the Gershonites within the tribe of Levi. He and his colleagues - the "trained singers of God" chosen by David and his generals to prophesy "with lyre, harp and cymbal" - had 288 descendants. (It's a loaded number, by the way, as I briefly mentioned above: 288 is precisely four times the original number of seventy-two elders described by Scripture as constituting the original prophetic caste as ordained by Moses.)

And what did these new prophets do? They "sang in the House of the Lord." They uttered prophecies "for the greater glory of God" (assuming that's what "raising a horn as a seer" means in this context.) Even for our taciturn Scriptures, it isn't much to go on.

There are some other few details worth mentioning, however. Asaph is specifically counted, for example, among the musicians who played when David first brought the Ark of the Law to Jerusalem - his instrument was the bronze cymbal - and, alone among his peers, his descendants are listed as the singers who returned from exile in Babylon. That's basically how the Chronicler depicts the man for us - as an ancient prophetic functionary whose songs were still in vogue in the days of King Hezekiah a dozen generations after his death and whose descendants survived to bring the musical traditions of pre-exilic Israel into the post-exilic age.

That passage, by the way, the one that mentions that the hymns of Asaph were still being sung centuries after his own lifetime specifically connects Asaph with David - whose songs were also still in vogue all those years later - almost as though there were special profundity in this particular parallel in the afterlife of their musical oeuvres. Furthermore, Asaph is the only one of his colleagues to have his name linked specifically to David's in that way by the Chronicler. I'm not sure if Nehemiah lived before or after the Chronicler, but he - Nehemiah - made the same point in his diary, noting specifically that the musical organization of Temple already existed "in the days of David and Asaph."

Whether Asaph, Jeduthun and Heman really served as court prophets in David's time or whether the Levitical clans that flourished - when they weren't being denounced, trapped, kidnapped or ambushed - in the Chronicler's day simply liked to imagine that their pedigree was unassailable because their ancestors had been personally chosen by David, the original singing prophet of Israel, cannot be known with any certainty. But what matters to me isn't whether the tradition is historically accurate, but what it meant to the men and women who believed it. And, by extension, what it can mean to those of us drawn to its latter-day contemplation all these centuries later.

The eightieth psalm is one of twelve psalms in the Psalter ascribed to Asaph. The poem is remarkable in its openness: it is the mystic Levite's formal plea for God to appear, to be seen, to be known. His language is remarkably open: *yoshêv hakkeruvim hofi'ah*, he commands half imperiously and half solicitously, "Appear, You Who are enthroned on the cherubs." Again and again, he returns to the same, amazingly unguarded refrain: "Illuminate Your face so that we (may see it and) be saved."

Although this poet writes as Asaph instead of David, he

appears to be no less miserable than his "David" colleagues in song. A third of his daily drink is made up of his own tears. His neighbours hate him. His enemies treat him with open contempt. When he writes of Israel as a vine *once* tended by God, but now left to fend for itself as marauders breach the wall once built to protect it, passers-by help themselves to its fruit, wild pigs gnaw at its tendrils, beasts feed on it and malicious villains burn its runners at will, no one can fail to be moved by both the pathos *and* the bitter force of the poet's lament.

This Asaph is very, very unhappy. Indeed, he would have to cheer up considerably for us to characterize him as *merely* despondent. The poet is as miserable as the other poets whose words we've been reading...but his misery doesn't really fit the situation of the Jewish people in the time of David when the Chronicler's Asaph lived. We know so little about the history of Judah in the first post-exilic centuries that it's hard to say if it fits the situation that pertained in the author's day, but I wonder if it isn't possible that the poet is only *formally* talking about the people Israel anyway, but really has himself and his own friends in mind. Are *they* the real Israel? Are *they* the true vine that has its roots deep in the quest for the living God? Are *they* the ones to whom God might reasonably choose to appear *because of* (not despite) the humiliation they've had to suffer at the hands of their priestly masters, those dry-as-dust functionaries and pedants whose idea of communing with the divine was slaughtering barnyard animals and roasting their flesh and fat so that God, somehow placated by the savory smell, would deign to make it rain?

The commentators all find ways to make the psalmist's words mean something other than what their literal meaning would appear to imply. For Rashi, "Appear!" means "Show Your might!" The Meiri starts off promisingly by noting that the poet refers to God as He Who is Enthroned Upon the Cherubs because that place above all others - the small spot between the wings of the golden cherubs sculpted onto the golden cover of the Ark of the Covenant - is the most propitious place in all existence for human beings to enter into a state of prophetic communion with God. Then, having said that, he withdraws to safer ground and writes that "Appear!" means "Watch over us!" rather than "Let us see you!" (As second best, he offers Rashi's interpretation.)

I personally see no reason to take the poet's words to mean anything other than what they mean literally. The poet's life was given to the quest for communion with God, a communion he defined (for whatever reasons) sensually rather than (merely) intellectually. He wanted God to appear before his eyes. He wanted God to illuminate His face so that he, the poet, and his friends might see it. Since they gathered at night in the Temple courtyard (I think) to engage in this kind of mystic endeavour, the light was a necessary additional request. Is this what another poet meant when he wrote in a different psalm that we can only see (real) light in the divine light of God - that we can only see God when He appears to us somehow (but potently) illuminated in His own light? When the poet calls on God to look down from heaven and see the suffering His faithful must endure, does he mean to say that God actually dwells in the sky and cannot, therefore, be seen by human beings below no matter how strong their wish to enter into an ongoing state of visual communion with God might be?

I think he means to say just the opposite: God dwells in heaven, but He does take note of those people below who seek Him ... of them *and* of their suffering *and* of the humiliation they must endure from the less enlightened. But this is not as irrational a divine quirk as it might at first sound, since it is also possible that He allows them to endure their suffering, perhaps, for a profound reason: because only a broken heart can divest itself of arrogance to the extent necessary to know God even cursorily, much less intimately. God does indeed dwell in heaven, then, but He also exists, tenuously, theoretically, perhaps even only *potentially* between the golden wings of the cherubs atop the Holy Ark. His invisibility is neither a self-imposed penance nor is it an absolute characteristic of God; it is merely the garb God wears when He comes calling, no more and no less. And, of course, there *was* no ark in the Holy of Holies in the Second Temple. It disappeared either prior to the fall of Jerusalem or else into the maelstrom caused by the destruction itself, so those who sought to hear God's voice had no golden cherubs' wings to use as access points to the divine realm *regardless* of whatever theory of divine communicativeness was motivating or inspiring them. They had, therefore, to improvise ...

And, in our day, must God be similarly dressed in His cloak of invisibility when the faithful come calling on Him, when the truly pious below devote their lives to the quest for the love of the God of Heaven? A hoary rabbinic tradition interprets an obscure couple of words in the Book of Kings to mean that the tradition that the cherubs atop the ark were a male and a female did not simply mean that one cherub of each gender was depicted, but that they were actually sculpted as a male and a female embracing each other in the throes of passion. I've always liked that idea, not least of all because its daring eroticism makes such a mockery of the flaccid piety of those who seek to know God without experiencing His presence. And the idea might well have appealed to the author of the eightieth psalm who chose to write behind the persona of Asaph ben Berekhiah, an individual - Asaph, not the poet - who presumably knew quite well how the cherubs were depicted in their silent stance over the box that held the only tangible vestiges of the divine revelation left in a world too busy or bored to seek anything more than formal meaning in it, let alone to seek communion with the Revealer Himself.

Perhaps "Appear!" means "Reveal Yourself!" - but, at least in this context, not through Your word (or rather, not solely through Your word) and not through the awesome concentration of Your power between the wings of the cherubim (which, at any rate, disappeared either before or during the exile in Babylon) and not even through the (divinely inspired) ability some individuals below have to believe wholeheartedly in a God they can neither see nor hear - but "Reveal Yourself!" in the way that ordinary people, people for whom seeing is believing and hearing is believing, in a way such people can fathom. And so we have our fifth clue: to see God you only need one thing other than God being present in the first place and that is for Him to illumine His face. (How can that not be true?) The trick, as ever, is knowing how to earn the right, how to acquire the merit, how to *provoke God to exist in the context of your specific life* without being so offensively provocative as to have precisely the opposite effect from the one you are seeking ....

13. *Mitziyyon 'Elohim Hofi'a*

He came. Or maybe He did.
The fiftieth chapter of the Psalter is also an Asaph psalm. And it begins with a startling assertion: that God indeed appeared to the poet. It's a bit ambiguous - the Hebrew word *hofi'a* is the same word I translated as a command when we were discussing the eightieth psalm - but although the past tense and the imperative in classical Hebrew aren't identical in every declension (just in some, and then only for certain verbs), the context here can easily be read to suggest that the poet is describing something that had actually happened. In real life.

Now, let's suppose I'm right about the tense. (And don't worry about the eightieth psalm coming after the fiftieth in the book as it's come down to us since there is no reason to assume the psalms are presented in the order in which they were written.) What actually did happen? God spoke. Aloud. (If that's what the poet means when he says that God summoned the whole world to this event–that any who were present at the right moment would have heard the voice, not just those who had cultivated the experience of hearing it from within the depths of their personal spiritual ability to know God.) He appeared from somewhere within the Temple–perhaps from where the cherubs' wings once were–which is why the poet has to assert that the voice was distinct and loud: the Levites weren't permitted to enter the innermost sanctum and would only have seen or heard God from a certain distance if it was there that He chose to appear or to declaim His word. He came in a whirlwind of fire and light. He called specifically for those of His faithful who served in the Temple to gather together that He might tell them His awful truth: that He's bored, perhaps even slightly irritated, by the whole sacrificial system. That He doesn't get hungry. Or thirsty. And that, in any event, He doesn't eat the flesh of the sacrificial bulls or drink the goat blood the priests spend their lives pouring out on the altar as libation offerings. That what He wants is *neither blood nor fat* ... but to be sought. What solace for one who seeks to hear such words not from the mouth of like-minded co-religionists, but from God Himself! And what awful tidings for those for whom religion is rule and rule book, for those to whom worship is obedience rather than love....

And then we come to the really bad news. The priests are wicked men who have forgotten God entirely, men the origin of whose right to teach others the rules of worship even God Himself can't quite recall. Worse, they are thick with the city's thieves and openly friendly and welcoming of adulterers into the sacred precincts - and the implication is *not* that they are reaching out to the sinners of the world to draw them back onto the right path. Worse than the company they keep, they gossip publicly about others - even their own brethren - and slander them without the slightest hesitation or moral compunction. And who specifically are these brothers on whose behalf the poet is so righteously indignant? Could they be the Levites themselves, those latter-day proponents of prophetic Judaism for whom worship was communion as much as libation and sacrifice?

There's a hint that the Levitical poet had just that interpretation in mind in that he finishes up his report on the oracle he received during his nighttime vigil by saying that, of all the sacrifices offered to God, the single one that actually appeals to Him is the thanksgiving offering called the *todah* sacrifice. Was there some special connection between the Levites and the *todah*?

In the Torah of the priests, the *todah* was merely another sacrifice, a sub-category of the wellbeing offering that could be offered up for a variety of different reasons. But we have a remarkable account in the personal diary of Nehemiah ben Hakhaliah that specifically links the Levites of the post-exilic period to the *todah*. Nehemiah is one of the most sympathetic characters in the whole of Biblical history, I think, and one of the most interesting. This isn't the place for a long biographical sketch, but the short of it is that he was the fellow that was sent with the blessings of the Persian hierarchy to Jerusalem in the middle of the fifth century B.C.E. with the mandate of getting the walls of the city (and as much of its decrepit infrastructure as he could manage) repaired and rebuilt. He kept a diary, which is the longest and most moving work of its kind in the Bible. And it's in his account of the ceremony that marked his successful reconstruction of the city walls of Jerusalem that he mentions the Levites and their special relationship to the *todah* sacrifice.

I suppose I should let Nehemiah speak for himself. *At the dedication of the wall of Jerusalem,* he writes, *the Levites, wherever they lived, were sought out and brought to Jerusalem to celebrate a joyful dedication with thanksgiving sacrifices* (Hebrew: todot) *and song, accompanied by cymbals, harps and lyres. The companies of singers assembled from the plains surrounding Jerusalem - from the Netophathite towns and from Beth Hagilgal and Sedoth Geva and Azmavet, for the singers had build themselves a series of towns around Jerusalem - and the priests and the Levites purified themselves as well as the rest of the people and the gates of the city and its wall. I had the officers of Judah go up onto the wall and I appointed two large* todot *(the plural of* todah*) and processions. One of these marched south on the wall to the Dung Gate, followed by Hoshaiah and half the officers of Judah ... and some of the young priests with trumpets ... and from there, they proceeded to the Fountain Gate, where they ascended the steps of the City of David directly before them ... and onward to the Water Gate on the east. The other* todah *marched on the wall in the opposite direction with me and half the people behind it ... and they halted at the Gate of the Prison Compound. Both* todot *halted at the House of God. And then the singers gave forth, with Yizrahiah conducting. On that day, they* (presumably the priests) *offered great sacrifices* (presumably the *todot*) *and they* (presumably everybody else present) *rejoiced, for God made them rejoice greatly; the women and children also rejoiced and the rejoicing in Jerusalem could be heard from afar.*

Now the meaning of the text rests in no small part on the meaning of the words *todah* and *todot*. It's usual to take them to refer to "thanksgiving choirs", an otherwise unknown usage of the term to refer to an otherwise unknown institution. I think it far more likely that the animals sacrificed that day were *todah* sacrifices - this *was* a festival of thanksgiving, after all - and that the word either refers to the oxen themselves or to the team of Levites that accompanied them to the altar. (And, if it does refer to a choir after all - then surely it would be to the choir whose songs accompanied the sacrifice after which it was named!) In either event, the point has been made forcefully in recent years that the Jerusalem Temple was basically a sanctuary of silence - to use Israel Knohl's felicitous phrase - but the *todah*-thanksgiving sacrifice appears to have been the great exception.

Whether the sense was that deep feelings of gratitude could only be stirred by music designed to accompany the slaughter of the sacrificial animals or if there was some sort of sense that the *todah* sacrifice required Levitical participation for some now forgotten reason, the basic idea is still that there was something peculiarly (and uniquely) Levitical about the thanksgiving sacrifice in the post-exilic period ... and that is how I would like to explain the assertion made by the poet at the end of the fiftieth psalm to the effect that God is more angered than pleased by the elaborate sacrificial structure developed over centuries within the priestly circles of old Jerusalem. The poet's contempt for the whole ritual world of sacrifice and libation is palpable, but he is prepared to make one single exception for the *todah* sacrifice, which he imagines that God continues (or rather, continued in his - the poet's - day) to find deeply satisfying: *But someone who offers a* todah *sacrifice - that person is truly honouring Me ... and it's to that individual -* and not to any of those pretentious fools who think that sacrifice and ritual can have meaning outside of the quest for communion with Me - *that I will show My face.*

Other psalmists felt just as strongly about the matter, by the way. The author of the fifty-first psalm, for example, is practically quoting Hosea when he writes that the only true sacrifice - or at least the only one God will favour in this woefully pre-messianic age - is the worshipper's broken heart divested (for once) of its arrogance and pointless pride. And the author of the fortieth psalm is at least echoing Jeremiah when he categorically denies the authenticity of priestly tradition by insisting that God neither asked for nor takes any pleasure in the ritual sacrifices offered to Him as part of the priestly worship service. The point is not so much that sacrifices are bad or good, merely that they, like all rituals, are empty vessels that can be filled up with whatever sentiments the worshipper brings to them ....

And so we come to our next clue: the rituals of worship are intended to give form, even substance, to the journey towards God. When undertaken with the right spirit, the act of pouring out the blood of a slaughtered ox on the altar - or, for that matter, of lighting Sabbath candles or of eating matzah *on Passover - can be a wonderful spur towards creating the kind of closeness to God that is the essential prerequisite to faith rooted in knowledge, even in love,* rather than in the fear of punishment. But ritual performed even according to the most exacting rules is utterly meaningless, perhaps even blasphemous, when undertaken for reasons other than the worship of God. That much seems unassailable ... but whether the concept of worshipping God itself can have meaning outside of the quest for the kind of intimate, experiential communion with God that is by definition as highly idiosyncratic as it is personally profound is not at all obvious ... unless it is. And how does one embark on this journey towards God? I suppose the same way one embarks on any journey ... by lifting up one foot and placing it further ahead on the path one has chosen than it was before one lifted it up ... just as the thanksgiving oxen marched along the walls of Jerusalem towards the Temple, the seat of the concentrated, palpable presence of God on this sorry earth....

14. *'Anêni*

One-sided conversation is not exactly revered by most people as the pinnacle of dialogic art. Indeed, for most people, having a one-sided conversation is as intensely annoying as it is informationally unsatisfying: the whole point of dialogue is that it be carried on not only with an ear that listens, but with a voice that talks back in response. The word "dialogue" itself implies this and common sense demands it; the word spoken into the void is widely damned as wasted breath not because it bears no meaning, but because its meaning is non-provocative in the sense that it fails to provoke a partner in dialogue to speak in response.

Except in prayer. Plenty of people who would never chat for twenty minutes with a busy signal - or worse, a dial tone - spend countless hours in prayer without (as far as I can tell) actually expecting the Almighty to answer. Some people I know, bound to the concept of prayer but offended by the apparent refusal of God to respond to their prayers in the normal way, insist that God actually does speak to them, but in a secret, interior way that only they can perceive. It's a neat solution - in a certain sense, it's the only plausible solution to a theological dilemma that would otherwise be relatively insoluble - but it isn't especially satisfying, especially to those of us hearing about it second-hand. (And remember what happens in our world to most people who hear voices in their heads - other than the voice of God, of course - that no one else can hear.)

The ancients, for all that their world was different from ours in terms of its outer trappings, dealt with the same problems of theology and metaphysics we moderns do. They prayed to the same God and puzzled over His perplexing, slightly irritating, possibly even humiliating silence. Some of the prophets themselves appear to have opted for plan B - I suppose that the underlying assumption resting just beneath all those countless passages in which the prophets of Israel tell the people what God has spoken unto them has to be that no one but the prophet *actually* heard the word of God when it was *actually* spoken and that no one but the prophet, therefore, was in a position to proclaim it accurately. But others of the prophets - and especially the latter-day Levites of the post-exilic period whose hymnal was our Psalter - appear to have wished to transcend Elijah's famous voice of silence (that is, the inner voice that prompted Elijah to know what it was God wanted of him) and to seek the ultimate in dialogue: the actual, spoken voice of the other in response to their own actual, spoken utterances.

I don't know what single word appears the most often in the Book of Psalms, but it might as well be *'anêni*. Over and over, in poem after prayer after hymn after song, the authors of the various psalms actually dare to call upon God to answer them. *'Anêni* means "Answer me!" (The plural form *'anênu* means "Answer us!" but is far less common.) Must we assume that these words were intended by the many different authors in whose poems they appear to refer to a communicative experience other than the one people generally intend them to denote when they say them, usually *in a certain tone*, to inattentive children? I suppose one *could* argue that ... but I'm not sure what arguments would truly persuade. When I, for one, tell my kids to answer me, I mean for them to respond in the normal way, in words rather than obscure gestures or thought patterns or subtle wrinkles in the natural pattern of being ....

It's a *bona fide* prophetic cry, this *'anêni*. Elijah, Scripture reports, used it at Mount Carmel and God hopped right to it, responding to the prophet's command with fire from heaven so intense that it consumed not only the bull sacrifice the prophet had prepared, but the altar the bull was resting on as well, stones and earth and wood included, and *also*, just to make the point even more forcefully, the moat Elijah had dug around it and filled with water. It wasn't much of a dialogic response - but Elijah, he of the voice of silence, seems to have been quite satisfied with it. Perhaps it suited Elijah for God to respond in the language of action rather than with human speech, but the Psalter, for whatever reason, simply takes the word and leaves the context behind. (Elijah's opponents, the prophets of Baal, use the same word in a slightly different form (*'Anênu*, "Answer us!") to call upon their god, by the way. And although they were *behaving* like priests, Scripture refers to them only as prophets. The narrator, I think, then portrays them using the vocabulary of prophecy to make his point even stronger.)

It wasn't an idle cry, either. Or at least it wasn't for *some* of the psalmists. Because, although the specific psalms in which the poets call upon God to answer them were composed (I suppose) as the liturgical part of the process of provoking mystic communion with the godhead, there are many other passages in the psalms in which God actually speaks directly to the poet. The poet, then, taking the role of public prophet, reveals the words of God to his (contemporary) listeners and (latter-day) readers.

As befits a book of prophecy provoked rather than endured, the Psalter mostly presents the oracles of God as short bursts of ecstatic inspiration. Hardly any long, complex prophetic speeches grace the twelve and a half dozen chapters of psalms that have come down to us. Instead we have the various pronouncements, messages and oracles that the mystics of the post-exilic period felt inspired (in both senses of the word) to report to others as the word of God.

One might well ask who these others were to whom they wished to communicate the stuff of their prophetic communion with God. It's actually a far more difficult question than it sounds like it ought to be because, by asking it, we are really asking to know the identity of the people for whom the psalms were written. Assuming they weren't composed as time capsules intended to bear news and information about the time and place of their composition to interested parties dozens of generations in the future - which is precisely how we generally relate to them - then why precisely *were* they composed?

Undoubtedly, there are different answers for different psalms. But I think I can discern three larger groups of poems in the Psalter. (Remember that although the Book of Psalms was the hymn book of the Second Temple, there's no question that some of the poems in it were older songs resurrected for contemporary use. Others, probably the majority, were more likely composed specifically for use in the Temple. For what it's worth, there are hardly any citations of passages from the Psalms in any of the authentic pre-exilic books of the Bible.)

One group is undoubtedly made up of songs that were sung by the Levites in their capacity as Temple singers, but which played no role in their self-perceived role as latter-day proponents of the religion of the pre-exilic prophets. The so-called royal psalms probably fall into this category - hymns that either actually do derive from the days when Israel was ruled by kings or else which are simply intended to be nostalgically evocative of the monarchy of pre-exilic times - as do probably the psalms specifically labelled as "Songs of the Steps" which tradition recalls as songs the Levites sang during public sacrifice as they stood on the steps that led up from the Court of Women to the Court of Israel in the Second Temple.

A second category is made up of those songs we have been discussing, hymns which I think were used as part of the nighttime ritual designed to provoke ecstatic experiences of personally seeing or hearing God.

The third category would be made up of hymns based on previous experiences of divine communion, songs that incorporated prior revelations as appropriate meditative stuff for subsequent efforts to provoke the same kind of experience that yielded the words or images being used in the first place. This is a bit complicated, but if I'm right, then this is only the earliest example of just that use of previously acquired mystic content in later Jewish hymnody. (Indeed, the fabulously rich hymnals of the so-called *merkavah* mystics of rabbinic times were filled with songs composed according to precisely the same principle of using the stuff of previous revelation as the meditative focus of subsequent attempts to provoke ecstatic communion with God.)

Partially because of the nature of the Hebrew language, it isn't always clear which psalms belong to which category. When the author of the twelfth psalm, for example, writes that the Lord says that He will now rise up to respond to the cries of the needy, it isn't that obvious (at least not to me) whether he is reporting actual words he heard God say to him in the context of prophetic communion or if he is merely waxing poetic in order to warn the oppressors of the poor in the name of God to desist from their tyrannization of the destitute. Other passages are equally difficult to interpret. The last three verses of the ninety-first psalm quote God in the first person, but could be taken as part of the poet's conception of what God *would* say about those who revere Him properly as easily as an actual revelation of the divine voice. On the other hand, when the author of the seventy-fifth psalm declares God's presence to be near and then segues neatly, almost seamlessly, into a first person oracle spoken by God, it's hard to imagine that the poet didn't expect his readers to presume that the substance of that oracle was vouchsafed to him in the context of some sort of prophetic experience of the divine.

This isn't a textbook on the psalms, so I don't feel obliged to discuss every verse in the book that could conceivably be taken as an oracle of God vouchsafed to a latter-day Levitical prophet. (I will, however, return to several of these passages in the next chapters.) Indeed, the point is merely this: when the poet wrote "O God, do not be silent, do not hold aloof, do not be quiet, O God", I don't think it's necessary (or reasonable or even especially desirable) to assume that his words must be assigned anything other than their simple meaning. No more than that, perhaps ... but certainly also no less!

The only thing more absurd than the thought that God might deign to speak to us as individuals *is the assumption that God lacks the will or, God forbid, the ability to speak at all. If there is a God and if He spoke once to his faithful, then it only seems reasonable to imagine that He will speak to His faithful again. So, however much we wish it to be, the problem is neither one of learning how to hear or even to listen. (Don't you know how to listen to someone speaking to you? Except for my children, doesn't everyone?) Those are after-the-fact excuses designed by the embarrassed pious to explain why their once garrulous God has fallen silent. I suppose that it's to their credit that they at least feel slightly embarrassed by the silence of God. But that's hardly enough...and the only real possibility of engaging in dialogue with the divine realm lies in learning to hear God when He speaks. Not to perceive divinity in the gnarly bark of an ancient oak or in the pristine stillness of a mountain lake at dawn. Not to hear the voice of God in a newborn's cry or in a lover's tender words. Not to denigrate the whole concept of divine speech by claiming to hear it where there is neither overt divinity nor, for that matter, actual speech of any real sort at all. But simply to hear God speak ... as one individual might speak with another. As the prophets heard Him. As Scripture assures us the whole people once did manage to hear Him. As we all need to believe possible if we are to truly believe in the existence of a communicative God in the first place ....*

15. *Zeh Hasha'ar*

> ... because this gate was
> only meant for you ...
> Kafka

The author of the 118th psalm hides behind neither David nor Asaph nor any other personality of the pre-exilic period. Perhaps for that reason, the rabbis of the Talmudic period debated whether this particular poem was created with reference to the past - as an expression of gratitude to God for David's successes - or as an oracle regarding the future. Modestly, I propose an alternative to both views: the poet is describing neither the future nor the past, but the present, *his* present.

In his own way, he's in as sorry a state as the authors of most of the other psalms I've written about. He's in intense distress. He perceives himself to be surrounded by fiends and villains on all sides. His enemies are all over him like a swarm of angry bees. He's learned better than to place whatever trust he can still muster in any mortal, even (probably he would say especially) in people of renown. But in the midst of all that detachment and alienation and misery and unhappiness, he calls on God and - amazingly enough - God answers him. And that experience, he says, brings him the relief he so desperately needs from the oppression of the world.

He doesn't tell us what God said. But the experience wasn't one of delightful intimacy as the uninitiated reader might expect it to have been. Just to the contrary, hearing God's voice was so intense an experience as to be almost painful. It sounds odd to hear the attainment of mystic communion with God described as pain, but the reality was apparently that the poet simply felt stretched to the limit of his endurance by the experience of hearing God speak - the word he uses is used elsewhere in Scripture to describe the kind of torture administered by evil taskmasters with whips and scorpions - but God did not hand him over to death - which he apparently half expected - and, in the end, he survived the experience at least long enough to write about it.

And now he is prepared to praise God precisely *because* He answered him - and not, God forbid, because of what it turned out to mean for a human being to suffer the experience of hearing the voice of God.

"This is the gateway to God," the poet declares triumphantly, setting aside his angst for a moment and exulting in the sheer triumph of having achieved communion with God in the style of the old time prophets *no matter how blurred the boundary between the pleasure of knowing God and the pain of hearing God may have been*. But this kind of intense communion is not for everybody. The gate may indeed exist, he continues, foreshadowing Kafka, but "the *tzaddiqim* alone may step through it."

And who, one may logically ask, are these *tzaddiqim*, these righteous individuals whom the psalmist allows may alone step through the gate towards God? The traditional commentators take the verse to refer to the righteous of any age, to the pure of motive and punctilious of observance whose faith is a function of (and a reward for) their piety as much as *vice versa*. But I wonder if there might not be a level here at which the word could be taken to refer specifically to the proponents of Levitical post-exilic prophetic Judaism. *They* are the ones, after all, who I believe actually did step through the gate to see and hear God ....

The *tzaddiqim* are mentioned as a group in more than a dozen psalms. And reference is made to individual *tzaddiqim* in another half-dozen texts. We've already had a chance to look at the 140th psalm, which concludes with the assertion that the *tzaddiqim* will be rewarded for their goodness and uprightness by being permitted to dwell "with the face of God." But what are we to make of the almost amazingly open comment in the 125th psalm to the effect that the staff of the wicked will never come down so totally on the backs of the *tzaddiqim* so as to send them packing entirely? These *tzaddiqim* certainly sound like the authors of the other psalms we've investigated, individuals all who felt persecuted by proponents of a kind of religion other than the one they themselves were promulgating as the key to communion with God.

The neo-prophets whose hymnal was our Psalter must indeed have felt that they had found the gateway to God. Did they feel a certain kinship to Father Jacob, the man who awoke after his vision at Bethel to exclaim in wonder that he had somehow found the gateway to heaven in that place? I've already suggested that they may well have, especially if the obscure reference to the name of the patriarch in the twenty-fourth psalm is correctly to be taken as a reference to a particular conventicle of specific individuals devoted to the search for God.

And what did they find when they passed through the portal to the celestial realm? They found a God who occasionally allows Himself to be seen. They found a God who speaks (at least sometimes) when spoken to. They found a God who takes responsibility for having made human beings such that we believe what we see and hear in a different and far more profound way than what we must merely conceptualize intellectually without the benefit of sensual stimuli to help us along. But these details pale in comparison to the larger, far more awesome point: that they actually did find God by stepping through the gate once specifically reserved for the tzaddiqim and now, we can only hope, for those who seek God honestly and forthrightly and in the context of absolute spiritual integrity. And where precisely is this gate to be found? That, after all, and not "where is God?" is the real question to ask. The good news is that the gate exists. The bad news is that it exists for each individual individually, privately, and totally, utterly idiosyncratically ... and for nobody else. No one will ever find his or her private gate by contemplating the spiritual successes of others in establishing their lives in God or in finding their own private gateways to God. You can admire such people. You can even emulate them, but to find God, you must step through the gate that exists for you alone ....

16. *Sefat Lo' Yada'ti 'Eshma'*

The Book of Psalms is a book of prophecy as studded with the remnants of prophetic experience as it is infused with the aftermath of spent prophetic passion. The authors of the psalms knew that it was possible not only to know God, but even to see him *despite* the stern warnings of the priestly tradition against daring to attain communion with the divine on such an intensely intimate level. They knew that the splendid light of God's presence - the light of His face, as they so often dared to call it - was there waiting to be accessed by the spiritually adept below who had both the nerve *and* the stamina to seek to love God in a sensual, real way rather than being content with the warm afterglow of prayer earnestly said or ritual activity zealously carried out. They understood revelation to be a concept that exists at many levels ... and they understood, logically, that the private oracle whispered into the ears of the pious during a nighttime vigil in the Temple courtyard was neither inherently nor necessarily less authentic than an experience of revelation carried out at the national level in the presence of millions.

The story of Israel at Sinai had, in the meantime, become the foundation myth of the Jewish people, the story that gave meaning and substance to the Jews' sense of themselves as an *'am segulah* and a *goy qadosh* - a treasured people, apart from the world and holy unto God. But in the post-exilic period, the word *qadosh* meant different things to different people. In the Torah, it is a synonym for priestly - which is why the phrases *mamlekhet kohanim* ("a kingdom of priests") and *goy qadosh* ("a holy nation") are used as parallel terms in the nineteenth chapter of Exodus. For the Chronicler, however, it was the Levites especially who were called holy, as the Chronicler's use of the word *qadosh* in the version of the prayer he puts in the mouth of King Josiah demonstrates. And, if the Psalter was (as we have been positing) *their* hymnal, then it was those same Levites, or at least some groups among them, whose holy work consisted of actually hearing the word of God spoken and gazing at that which the priests taught no one may look at and live.

And what did God say when He deigned to speak? In the twelfth psalm, He says that He will arise (either from His throne or from His lethargy or perhaps from both) to bring redemption to the oppressed. In the thirty-second psalm, the psalm destined eventually to be designated for communal recitation on the Day of Atonement, He is heard to admonish His faithful to be neither like mules nor horses. (The poet cites God's own explanation of this rather gnomic thought: that although animals need bits and bridles to keep them going in the right direction, human beings should be sufficiently motivated by the desire to serve God so as not to need such artificial restraining devices.)

Sometimes the messages received are so obscure as to defy interpretation these many centuries later - we can only guess what it meant to the ancients to know that God had declared his intention to divide up the town of Shechem and personally survey the valley of Sukkot, as reported by the author of the sixtieth psalm and then repeated a second time for good measure in a different chapter in the Psalter. The references to Babylon and Rahab in the eighty-seventh psalm are equally obscure, but other oracles are as clear as they are pointed. When the author of the seventy-fifth psalm, for example, reports that God has determined to judge the world *equitably* at a time of His own choosing, for example, it isn't hard to imagine whom the Levitical poet was hoping to upset with that news.

Actually, any number of oracles preserved in the Psalter endorse the hostility the psalmists felt towards their detractors and enemies. I've already suggested that it could well have been the priests of their day - men whose brand of Judaism was so totally different in style and emphasis than the neo-prophetism of the psalmists - about whom they liked to imagine they were singing. The sixty-eighth psalm, for example, notes that God has specifically predicted that the tongues of the psalmists' dogs will have the opportunity one day to lap up the blood of their enemies. Other passages are equally blunt: the author of the 110th psalm, for example, quotes God as predicting that the enemies of the author's superior would end up as his personal footstool, presumably after being slaughtered and stuffed by some bloodthirsty taxidermist.

Other oracles are directed at the group of prophetic seekers themselves or at the entire Jewish people. They shouldn't be stubborn, stupid people who provoke God's anger *even though they have seen* (!) *the tangible, physically perceptible evidence of God's power.* They should be proactive and vigorous in their support of the poor. They should be kind to orphans. The should comport themselves in a way that reflects their faith that God judges each individual according to his or her own deeds. They should seek God's peace by avoiding foolishness.

Perhaps the most extended description of the ritual designed to provoke God into speaking is found in the eighty-first psalm, a poem attributed to Asaph. It is night, the night of the new moon. The sky, illuminated only by the thinnest sliver of lunar surface, is at its darkest. The proceedings are thus enshrouded beneath a blanket of semi-darkness as a hymn begins to the accompaniment of drums and harps. God is invoked in the song as the God of Jacob, the very patriarch elsewhere identified with those who seek the divine face, the man who found the gateway to heaven even though he knew not the true nature of the place in which he was when he first lay down there to sleep for the night.

Suddenly, the assembled hear a blast of the ram's horn, the same *shofar* that the Israelites heard at Sinai and which (then as now) signalled the onset of the communicative presence of God. And with that, God begins to speak. He speaks not in a human tongue - for how could the word of God ever be imprisoned in the grammar and vocabulary of any *specific* human language? - but in the language of the heart, of the soul. *Sefat lo yada'ti 'eshma'*, the psalmist relates, unsure how to describe an experience that transcends human language in normal words: I hear, he writes, speech encapsulated in a kind of speech I hadn't previously known to exist. And what kind of speech is it of which the mystic poet has never heard if not the *sefat 'emet* - "the language of truth" - that the author of a different Biblical book describes as the speech of eternity?

The assembled are hesitant at first: who are they, they wonder humbly, to hear the voice of God? To this, the poem itself responds with reference to history: the quest for God is as old as the flight from Egypt to Sinai ... and (presumably) as legitimate in any setting as in any other. Reassured, the seekers calm themselves as they begin to interiorize the spirit of prophecy and master the message being sent to them from God. They set their ritual paraphernalia aside - mysterious allusion is made to a basket or a pot of some sort that one seeker appears to have taken from the shoulder of another perhaps as a sort of ritual unburdening of the body meant to mirror (or provoke) the unburdening of the soul that must precede participation in this kind of intercourse with the divine realm - and prepare to know God.

God's first words are calming: "You have called upon Me in distress," God says, "but I shall grant you relief even as I answer you in a voice of thundering secrecy and test your mettle in the manner in which I tested your ancestors in the desert." (The words *sêter ra'am*, "thundering secrecy," could be translated in a variety of ways, but I think they probably refer to the inner voice of God the prophet hears with his heart and in his head rather than through his ears. Others, it is true, reported that the divine voice was audible to any and all who were, or who might have been, present, but this particular instance of neo-prophetic communion with the divine seems to have been centred on an intimate experience rooted within the perceptive powers of the individual rather than the group. Perhaps the poet is trying to find his own way of expressing the inner voice that the Biblical author who described the experiences of Elijah at Sinai could only think to call a voice of thin, barely existent silence.)

At any rate, the meaning is clear enough: the courage to hear the word of God has to be developed from within the seeker's own breast and is neither something to be sought as a gift from God nor something to be presumed automatically to exist. The ability to withstand the degree of intimacy with God that the mystic seeker seeks is itself a test ... and is, ultimately, the only true test of the mystic's mettle. But this is not a fool's path down which the prophet has begun to wander: if the prophet will only open his mouth, then God will fill it up with words of divine origin, with prophecy.

What comes next is a strange mixture of traditional and innovative information. Israel must obey God. Israel must worship no other gods - and especially not the gods of foreign nations. Israel must acknowledge God as the Master of History. The men and women of Israel must abandon the promptings of their own wilful hearts.

And then, presumably, the point: God will indeed crush the enemies of Israel, striking them again and again. Moreover, those who truly hate God will eventually end up cowering before Him, terrified before the prospect of eternal damnation and doom.

Given the constant emphasis in most of the psalms I have been discussing on the need for God to keep the mystics' enemies from mocking them or even from physically abusing them, I wonder if the prophetic word in the eighty-first psalm wasn't meant as a double-edged sword, one side of which could threaten the outer enemies of Israel at the same time the other edge intimidated the inner enemies of the true Israel, the faithful who sought God in the style of the old-time prophets and who actually succeeded, at least sometimes, in provoking the word of God.

I suppose either reading is possible - and it's certainly possible that both are correct - but the more important point to be gleaned from the eighty-first psalm is that honey can indeed come from the rock (as the poet notes in his closing strophe) and that mere human beings are not damned by their humanity as much as they are enabled (and ennobled) by it to seek God and to hear His voice.

Taken all together, the information we can glean from the eighty-first psalm is profound. Israel has an outer and an inner aspect. The outer aspect - based on blood and faith - endures as an ongoing monument to the role God plays in history, but the inner aspect - the one rooted in the unquenchable, (almost) undeniable desire every human being feels (or rather, may feel) to know God and to love God and to commune with God personally, idiosyncratically, privately and intimately - that aspect exists as well and may be nurtured and cultivated in any time and place. History, after all, doesn't limit the search for God in the future as much as it grants that noble quest legitimacy in all subsequent generations. And this too: one gets the impression that the psalmists' world basically consisted of two distinct groups of people: the one made up of those who sought God and the other, of their enemies. To the extent that their world is ours as well, then what other option (I might ask) do we have other than belonging to one group or the other? Looking at the situation logically, the only plausible answer would have to be: none at all.

Epilogue: *Lo Navi 'Anokhi*

> Seek God and live!
> Amos

There are always two ways.
The Torah devotes an enormous amount of time to discussing the great moveable sanctuary the Israelites constructed in the desert during their long years of wandering from slavery in Egypt to freedom in the Land of Israel. That sanctuary was called by a variety of names: *'ohel mo'ed* ("the tent of assignation" or "the tent of meeting"), *qodesh* ("the sanctum") and *mishkan* ("the tabernacle" or, more literally, "the dwelling"), all of which are used more or less interchangeably in Scripture. There are, however, four distinct passages in Torah in which the phrase *'ohel mo'ed* is used to designate something else, a desert sanctuary that appears *not* to be the *mishkan* and in which extraordinary things are said to have transpired. Although this might seem at first to be a mere issue of lexicography or literary style, there is a profound point to be made here and so it is precisely those four anomalous texts I would like now to consider.

The first consists of four verses in the thirty-third chapter of Exodus: *Now Moses would take the tent and pitch it outside the camp at some distance from the camp and he called it the 'ohel mo'ed ("the tent of assignation"), since it was to this tent, which was outside the camp, that any who sought God would repair. Now, the custom was that when Moses went out (of the camp) to (go to this) tent, the people would all rise to their feet and remain standing at the doorways of their tents and they would watch Moses until he arrived at the 'ohel. (The reason for this interest was that) when Moses would arrive at the 'ohel, a pillar of cloud would descend and stand at the* doorway of the 'ohel and talk with Moses. And when all the people would see the pillar of cloud standing at the opening of the 'ohel and they would rise and bow down, each individual at the doorway of his own tent. Then God would speak to Moses face to face, as one man would speak to another, after which Moses would return to the camp - but his servant Joshua bin Nun would never leave the 'ohel.

Although most of the commentators do their best to connect this passage to its larger context, these connections seem forced and, to a certain extent, motivated by ulterior considerations. Indeed, the fact that the text begins by speaking of Moses taking "*the* tent" implies that the text must originally have had a context in which the identity of that particular tent would have been clear - but that that context is not the chapter in which this passage appears in Scripture as it now stands. Still, the meaning of the passage is relatively clear even in the absence of its original context: Moses was bidden to set up a tent outside the camp which would serve as the locus of prophecy, the place at which the divine pillar of cloud would descend to earth to communicate the will of God either *just* to His prophet or to any Israelite who wished "to seek God" *through* the agency of His prophet.

There are several other passages in Scripture in which unmistakeable reference is made to this same tent. For example, in the eleventh chapter of Numbers, we read the following story: *And God said to Moses, "Gather for me seventy of Israel's elders ... and bring them out to the 'ohel mo'êd and set them up there with you. I will come down and speak to you there and draw off some of the (prophetic) spirit that is on you and I will put it on them so that they can share some of the burden of the people with you and you will not have to bear it alone" ... And Moses went out and reported the words of God to the people and gathered seventy of Israel's elders together and arranged them around the 'ohel. And God came down in a cloud and spoke to him and drew off of the spirit that was on him (i.e. on Moses) and put it on the seventy elders. And as it came to rest on them, they began to prophesy ... Two men, one named Eldad and the other Medad, had remained in the camp, yet the spirit rested upon them (also) - they were on the list (of elders who were supposed to go out to the tent), but they hadn't gone - and they prophesied in the camp. A lad ran out and told Moses, "Eldad and Medad are prophesying in the camp!" Joshua bin Nun, the one of the lads who was Moses' (actual) servant, responded to that by saying, "My lord*

Moses, arrest them!" But Moses said to him, "Are you jealous on my account? Would that all the Lord's people were prophets upon whom the Lord put his spirit!"

There can't be any real question that this tent is the same one that we found described in Exodus 33. For one thing, it is called *'ohel mo'êd*, just like in Exodus. For another, it is located outside rather than within the camp. Most significantly of all, it is described as precisely the same locus of prophecy: in Exodus, the Israelites in search of God would send Moses to the tent so God could speak to him through the guise of the pillar of cloud, while here, the elders are actually to be invested as prophets in Israel and the ceremony of investiture must logically take place in the locus of prophecy itself. Eldad and Medad are merely the exceptions that prove the rule - they are only worth mentioning in the first place because they prophesied within the camp where such activity did not generally take place. Even the cloud provides a link between the two texts, as it seems impossible to imagine that the pillar of cloud in Exodus and the cloud in Numbers are not meant to denote the same divine disguise.

Nor can there be any question of the identity of the tent mentioned in the very next chapter of Numbers. There, in the context of the story about Aaron and Miriam's dispute with Moses I've already mentioned a few times, we read the following details: *Suddenly, the Lord called to Moses, Aaron and Miriam, "Go out, all three of you, to the 'ohel mo'êd!" And the three of them went out. The Lord came down in a pillar of cloud and stood at the entrance of the 'ohel and called out "Aaron and Miriam!" And the two of them went out. And he said, "Hear my words! If a prophet among you be (truly) of God, then I can either appear to him in a vision or speak to him in a dream. But my servant Moses is not like that - he is the most faithful of all my (prophets). Mouth to mouth I speak with him and (I appear to him) visually, not in riddles. He gazes upon the image of God - so why do you not hesitate to speak against my servant Moses?*

The tent here has to be the same as in the other texts: it is called *'ohel mo'êd*, it is outside the camp ("go out, all three of you ...") and it serves as the locus of prophecy, the place in which God wishes formally to acknowledge Moses' prophetic superiority over the other prophets of Israel. Furthermore, the phrase *peh 'el peh* ("mouth to mouth") is clearly parallel to the reference in Exodus to God speaking to Moses "face to face."

The fourth text I wish to present in this context is taken from the thirty-first chapter of Deuteronomy: *And the Lord said to Moses, "Behold, your time to die has come. Call Joshua and (the two of) you stand at the 'ohel mo'êd that I might instruct him." And Moses and Joshua went and stood at the 'ohel mo'êd. And the Lord appeared at the 'ohel mo'êd in a pillar of cloud which stood at the opening of the 'ohel* ....

The tent here is certainly the same as in the other texts: it is called *'ohel mo'êd*, it is frequented by the pillar of cloud *and* by Moses and Joshua, just like in Exodus. And the context is the same as in Numbers: God is shifting the burden of prophecy from Moses' shoulders (there, in Numbers, partially; here, in Deuteronomy, entirely) and this can only be accomplished, or rather, can only properly take place at the focal point of Israelite prophetic endeavour: the *'ohel mo'êd*.

Now, as I mentioned above, there is another tent as well in Israelite tradition and it too has a variety of names, including *'ohel* and *'ohel mo'êd*. The most elaborate description of this other tent is in the twenty-fifth through twenty-seventh chapters of Exodus, but although the word *'ohel* is used repeatedly in the text to denote this sanctuary, the construction of which Scripture specifically attributes to Bezalel ben Uri and Oholiab ben Ahisamach, there can be no doubt that this *'ohel* is not the *'ohel* mentioned in the previous texts. For one thing, this *'ohel* is located inside the camp at its very centre, not outside. For another, it is the centre of priestly worship, not of prophetic communion, and therefore only the priests, Aaron and his descendants, may enter into its innermost precincts; there is almost no mention of Moses penetrating into this *'ohel*, much less of little Joshua (an Ephraimite!) actually dwelling there, either alone or in the company of the other lads.

Now there is a passage in the Book of Exodus that asserts that this inner sanctuary was *precisely* the place to which a prophet would have to repair to hear the voice of God booming out from between the wings of the cherubim sculpted atop the golden cover of the ark, but that's only so much priestly theory ... and the reality of the situation is that there is only one single verse in the Bible that specifically refers to Moses actually entering into this priestly sanctuary for the sake of experiencing the prophetic voice of God in that place. This latter reference, however, precise and unambiguous though it may be, is a solitary, anomalous, strangely contextless remark that can hardly be given the weight of an independent substantiating narrative and which is overridden anyway by the weight of tradition: when Scripture actually does offer a picture of Moses behaving like a working prophet - for example, when he turns to God for an answer to the specific question raised by the daughters of Zelophehad about the laws of inheritance or for divinely inspired information about how to deal with the issue of the people unable to celebrate the Passover by virtue of their personal impurity or for divine instructions about how to punish the public blasphemer or what to do with (or rather, to) the unfortunate man who was caught gathering sticks on the Sabbath - in those cases, the text is often suspiciously vague about where precisely it is that Moses retires to make his inquiries. There are, at any rate, no references to mercy-seats or cherubs' wings at any of these places, thus leaving readers to come to their own conclusions about the precise place it was to which Moses repaired "to bring their case - the case of Zelophehad's daughters - before the Lord (Numbers 27:5.)" And then, on top of all that, there are the specific instructions preserved in the priestly Torah to the effect that no one but the High Priest may enter the Holy of Holies (where the ark with its golden cherubim was to be installed) ... and even he is severely restricted as to when and under what circumstances he may go there. How, then, was Moses to feel free to drop in whenever any Israelite wished him "to seek God" on his or her behalf?

    Be all that as it may, this priestly *'ohel* has specific appurtenances which are discussed and described in Scripture in exquisite detail - but none of them, least of all the altars, has anything to do with the prophetic experience, thus leaving the priestly sanctuary singularly *un*suited to be named as the specific place to which the Levite Moses was instructed to go to hear the voice of divinity and to learn the precise answers to the specific questions he wishes to put to his God.

    How are we, then, to explain the fact that this inner-camp sanctuary, so often called *mishkan* or *qodesh* is also called *'ohel* and *'ohel moʻêd*?

    It is, I think, clear enough that Israelite tradition originally maintained two distinct traditions about desert sanctuaries. The Tent of Meeting, the *'ohel moʻêd*, was outside the camp and was recalled as having been the locus of prophecy and, as such, the domain of Moses. The Tabernacle, usually called *mishkan* or *qodesh*, but also *'ohel* and, occasionally even *'ohel mo'êd* was inside the camp and was the sacred centre of Israelite priesthood: the domain of Aaron. Later confusion surrounding the distinct nature of these traditions notwithstanding, it is clear enough that each of these shrines plays its own role in Israelite tradition. Together, they establish the unimpeachable cachet of desert provenance for both the priesthood and the institution of prophecy, the twin poles of ancient Israelite religious behaviour.

But we are peeking behind the scrim here - and the reality of the situation is that the text of the Torah as it has come down to us presents only one sanctuary to its readers, one single desert shrine that is called by a variety of different names and which appears to have once been two different and distinct things.

As I've remarked again and again, the Torah is a priestly document that reflects the spirituality and political positions of the priests of post-exilic antiquity. In *their* world, there was only one sanctuary. And it was in *their* world (or rather, in their world-view) that there were priests rather than prophets leading the people forward towards God. *Their* spirituality had overwhelmed and subsumed the spirituality of the prophetic caste of the ancients. And as for the Levites - slaves of the priestly caste, as the Torah itself repeatedly, if rather petulantly, insists - *their* pathetic midnight efforts to resurrect the spirituality of the prophetic caste of the pre-exilic kingdoms of Israel and Judah were barely existent, barely worth nodding towards ... just as Torah barely stops to nod to the tradition of a second sanctuary of prophecy located outside rather than deep within the camp of Israel.

The Psalter, the songbook of the ancient Levites, is riddled with poets' worries about being overwhelmed by hostile forces, foes too many to count who are out for blood constantly and in the greatest earnest, enemies who demand proof positive that the poet truly does know God and who are hardly going to be fobbed off with, of all pathetic things, poetry. And these aren't occasional observations, either. Indeed, there are scores upon scores of references to the poets' fears of suffering scorn and humiliation, even physical harm, at the hands of unnamed and unidentified villains throughout the Book of Psalms. I've cited some of these texts above, but the reader needs to realize that the Psalter is literally riddled with this kind of writing and that the fear of denunciation, public ridicule and physical assault is one of the two or three unifying themes that transform the disparate songs of the Psalter into a cohesive work.

Did the Levites fear being overwhelmed by adversaries selling a different kind of spiritual merchandise, a different method of seeking, of worshipping, of knowing and loving God? If the Psalter is their hymnal, then the answer certainly could be that that was *precisely* what they feared. And if the five-part Psalter of David was composed as a response to the five-part Torah of Moses, then the point can only have been to try to preserve a kind of ancient Judaism that risked being subverted, submerged and finally subsumed altogether by the institutionalized, cultic faith that had power, money and the inestimably grand authority of the Jerusalem high priesthood behind it.

Eventually, if only literarily, the sands of the Sinai began to cover the prophetic tent, the *'ohel mo'êd* to which "all who sought God would go." But the image became frozen in time when the text of Scripture was suddenly fixed in the very period of history we are discussing - and here and there, one can still see some few references to that sanctuary of prophecy peeking out from just behind and (occasionally) between the stately columns of the priestly Torah. Indeed, it was in this period that the priestly Torah became *the* Torah of all Israel or, as Scripture itself puts it, the Torah of God. The original nature of the Psalter was forgotten and the rabbis - for whom the Torah of Moses was the word of God in even the most literal (and least likely) sense of the term - found nothing in it even remotely hostile either to the spirituality of the Torah or to their own religious program. The memory of the desert sanctuary vanished *almost* entirely, but *not* entirely, continuing on to live in a real enough way for textual archaeologists to uncover, ponder and (at least in this author's case) admire millennia later.

The specific meaning of the various references to the specific practices in which the Levites engaged to awaken the visible or auditory presence of God in their midst were forgotten or dismissed as so much poetry or metaphor. Indeed, the ancient tradition the Levites must have cherished above all others - that tradition which affirmed the Levitical ancestry of the greatest of all prophets, Moses himself - seems to have been suppressed, if not quite submerged, by the authors of Scripture as it has come down to us. There are, at any rate, no references to Moses acting as a Levite *per se* in any Biblical story. Indeed, Scripture has God referring to Aaron as Moses' brother Levite, not the other way around! Now Aaron, of course, was also a member of the tribe of Levi. But by emphasizing that aspect of his pedigree rather than his status as progenitor of the priestly caste, Scripture is laying the groundwork for thinking of the Levites of the post-exilic period as junior priests rather than prophets, precisely as the priestly editors of the Torah would have no doubt liked everybody to think: the Biblical period hadn't even come to an end and already the sense was being created that the priests and their version of the ancient religion of Israel was the truly authentic one.

The tension between prophets and priests in post-exilic Judah was eventually no less forgotten than was the *real* point of the poet's wistful musing about how lovely it would be if brethren were only able to find the will (or would he have said the courage?) to sit down together in peace.

The books of the prophets were deemed so entirely in step with rabbinic theology that passages from them were selected and entered into the weekly lectionary cycle of Scriptural passages to be read aloud in synagogue as a kind of literary supplement to the weekly reading from the Torah itself. The word *torah* in the Psalter was deemed always to refer to *the* Torah of Moses, despite the fact that more or less every single one of the three dozen or so verses that feature the word (two thirds of which are in the 119th psalm, where at least one reference is to serving God precisely by abandoning his *torah*) is equivocal and could be referring just as easily to the *torah* of the prophets as to *the* Torah of the priests. (At any rate, when the psalmist wrote that he felt *torah* - the word itself means nothing more specific than "teaching" or "lesson" in Hebrew, a language without capital letters - when he felt the abiding presence of *torah* deep within his bowels, he was, I think, certainly referring (as he says more or less specifically) to a special, personal revelation intended by God specifically for him much in the same way the prophet Ezekiel spoke about how the personal scroll God sent him filled up *his* bowels or the prophet Jeremiah about the word of God churning and roiling in *his* troubled intestines.)

In every age, there have been those who have sought to know God intimately rather than merely to know *of* Him through the medium of other people's revelatory experiences. These are the people to whom Amos was speaking when he said, speaking in the name of God: *Seek ye Me and live.* The Hebrew words - *dirshuni viḥyu* - have a certain immediacy to them, a certain challenging cadence that resists translation. Seek Me and live - not *despite* the experience, but *because* of it. Seek Me and live - not by *remaining* alive, but by *becoming* alive. Not merely by being *not dead* as a result of journeying to God, but by being *alive* as a result of embracing life fully and specifically through the worship of its Author.

The context in Amos is telling. The prophet is a northerner and he speaks in a northern context and from a northern vantage point. He warns his countrymen *not* to seek God at Bethel or at Gilgal, two of the great holy sites of the northern kingdom, much less at Beersheba in neighbouring Judah. There are only buildings in those places, he means to say, conditionally holy sites that came into existence at a certain moment and which will eventually stop existing. Seek God and live, the prophet says, this time speaking in his own name. Seek God in His temple, he says, meaning that the faithful should not waste their time seeking the temple, but should rather devote themselves and their efforts to seeking the God whose worship the temple was built to inspire.

Amos had his run-ins with the official priesthood of his time and place in the person of one otherwise unknown priest named Amaziah who served in the northern sanctuary of Bethel. What the real cause of this Amaziah's problem with Amos was, I can't say. The whole passage is short and neither Amaziah nor Amos says all that much in it, but one thing Amaziah does insist is that he's learned of - without quite saying that he himself has heard - some seditious remarks the prophet has made about King Jeroboam. He tries to throw him out of the country, or at least out of Bethel which is, he notes pointedly, both a royally sponsored sanctuary and the site of the royal palace. The prophet is unimpressed. *Lo' navi' 'anokhi,* Amos says - he's not a prophet, at least not a professional member of the prophetic guild, and neither was his father one. What's more, he already has a job, he insists, actually more than one: he raises cattle and sheep and tends sycamore trees for a living. This prophet business is a temporary thing, Amos adds almost wearily - he was just minding his own business when God came unexpectedly to him and sent him to bear His word to Israel.

Although they don't cite it directly, the creators of the Book of Psalms must have liked that story, truncated though it might be in its Scriptural version. For they too were neither *nevi'im* nor *benê nevi'im*, neither "real" prophets nor members-in-training of the long-defunct prophetic guild of ancient Israel. Indeed, I see them as the first *non*-prophets who strove nonetheless to know God, to hear His voice, to see His face, to "come to the temple and to gaze on the beauty of the divine form". In a certain sense, they were the first Jewish mystics. If you ask me, they were also the first Jewish moderns.

We, in our world, are so used to dismissing efforts to perceive God sensually rather than merely intellectually as so much metaphor and hyperbole that it actually requires some degree of discipline to take such efforts seriously as authentic, pious acts and their practitioners (or attempters) as *bona fide* religious people whose spiritual work was (and is) legitimate, ancient and, at least in terms of its end goals, deeply traditional. It's a stretch for most of us who live out our spiritual lives within the complacent, smug world of organized Jewish life to consider - or even, for that matter, to remember - that there were once Jewish individuals for whom ritual was a tool rather than an end unto itself. And it's even more of a challenge to force ourselves to ponder the fact that, at the earliest stages of the transformation of Judah-ism to Judaism, there were *already* people opting out of the system - or at least choosing a distinctly different spiritual path - not in order to become free of God and His service, but to embrace both God *and* His service in a palpable, sensual way that corresponded then (as, indeed, it corresponds now) to what human beings *really* mean when they say that they know one another in the simple, unmysterious way in which ordinary people perceive, esteem and enjoy each other in friendship and love.

Like Amos - and certainly like the Levites of the post-exilic period - I am also neither a prophet nor the son of a prophet nor am I a member of the professional prophetic guild (now fallen several millennia even *further* into desuetude than it was in post-exilic Judah.) For better or worse, what I am is the product of twenty-two or three post-Biblical centuries of development and thought. My Judaism, therefore, cannot be what Judaism itself isn't. But it can be enhanced, perhaps even defined, precisely by considering what Judaism became in light of what it could have been. The priests of old won. Their Torah is our Torah and their faith, our religion. Their sanctuary became the desert shrine Scripture describes in such exquisite, one might almost say excessive, detail and it is *their* rituals, and no one else's, that became the commandments that bind all Jews to each other and to God.

Like all line drawings, the picture painted in this book is distinctly simpler than the actual reality behind it must have been. The vast majority of Jewish people in antiquity - Levites and priests and regular folks - were not fully in one camp or in the other, I don't imagine. They were somewhere on a spectrum, perhaps closer to one or the other of its ends, but nevertheless obliged - or rather, challenged by circumstance - to discover a way to balance two conflicting views of Jewish spirituality and to find some sort of reasonable way for them to co-exist within the same breast. The same could be said of us all: the vast majority of engaged, committed Jewish people today are *neither* dry-as-dust ritualists *nor* wild-eyed seekers of visual or auditory communion with the divine realm. Instead, they - we - fall somewhere on a spectrum between what Judaism is and isn't, between Pentateuch and Psalter, between Torah and *Tillim*, between the worship of God as Israel's end of the covenantal bargain that binds God and the Jewish people and the use of that same worship as a vehicle towards intimate, sensual, utterly personal communion with that same God.

Where do I personally stand in all of this? I ask that question aloud not because I intend to answer it publicly, but merely to show that it can be asked, perhaps even that it must be asked openly. The answer - the honest answer, as opposed to the knee-jerk response rabbis are trained to give - however, cannot be sought in books, even sacred ones, or in sermons ... but can only come from the deepest recesses of a specific individual's spiritual consciousness. From the secret source of the desire for God that animates and guides human life from cradle to grave. From the private heart to which the psalmist referred when he wrote the words *bekhol lêv yidreshuhu* - they shall seek Him wholeheartedly, which is to say: with *all* their hearts, with *all* its chambers, secret and otherwise, and with *both* of its sides.

Bibliographical Notes

[In the following notes, *BT* refers to the Babylonian Talmud and *PT* refers to the Palestinian Talmud. The acronyms by means of which the great medieval commentators are known are deciphered in the author's note at the beginning of this volume.]

Epigraphs: 1 Samuel 3:3; Mao Zedong as cited by Jan Wong in her *Red China Blues* (Toronto, 1996), p. 51; Sifri Deuteronomy to *parshat shoftim*, ed. Finkelstein (Berlin, 1939) §161; John Donne, from "Upon The Translation of the Psalms by Sir Philip Sidney, and the Countess of Pembroke his Sister" in *Complete Poetry and Selected Prose*, ed. John Hayward (London, 1930), p, 302; Psalm 119:62. The quotation from Elimelech Weissbrot is from the book *Midrash Elimelech* that I have been writing for the fictitious rabbi for at least a decade.

Author's Note: The Chronicler (i.e. the author of the Book of Chronicles) notes that both men and women served as singers in the First Temple at 1 Chronicles 25:5-6. Cf. the reference to female drummers at Psalm 68:26 and to female singers at Ezra 2:65 (=Nehemiah 7:67.) Are these singers identical to the maidens mentioned in the superscription to Psalm 46 (and possibly Psalm 9, cf. Psalm 48:15 and 1 Chronicles 15:20)? There may also be a slightly corrupted reference to female singers in the Temple at Amos 8:3, as noted by W.O.E. Oesterley in his *The Psalms in the Jewish Church* (London, 1910), p. 116.

Preface: The Torah refers to prophetic apostates at Deuteronomy 13:2-6 and to false prophets at Deuteronomy 18:20-22. The Torah notes that the none of the other prophets was Moses' equal at Numbers 12:6-8. The passage about a prophet "like Moses" appears at Deuteronomy 18:15-19. The Torah uses the word *navi'* ("prophet") to refer to Aaron at Exodus 7:1 and, in the feminine form, to Miriam at Exodus 15:20. The story in which God discusses the nature of prophecy with Miriam and Aaron is in Number 12. (For what it's worth, Abraham - who actually does see God and hear His voice - is called a prophet at Genesis 20:7.) The Bible says that God spoke to Moses the way "one man speaks to another" at Exodus

33:11. The Psalter refers to priests here and there, mostly in liturgical passages like Psalm 115:10, Psalm 118:3 or Psalm 135:19 or in poems like Psalm 132 that speak of the glory of the priesthood as a feature of ancient times. There are dozens of references to the Temple and its forecourts and various precincts throughout the Psalter, e.g. at Psalm 3:5, Psalm 5:8 Psalm 11:4, Psalm 26:8, Psalm 28:2, Psalm 29:9, Psalm 48:10, Psalm 84:4 and 11, Psalm 100:4 or Psalm 134:1. The Book of Psalms presents dismissive or disparaging verses about the sacrificial system of worship pursued by the priests of old Jerusalem at Psalms 16:4, 40:7, 50:8-13, 51:18-21, 69:31-32 to which prophetic passages such as Hosea 6:6 or Jeremiah 7:21-26 may be compared.

Chapter One: The rabbis note that people quote Scripture profusely when they have no idea how to answer a question is found in the Palestinian Talmud at Berakhot 2:3, 4c. The reference to the eleventh chapter of Deuteronomy is specifically to Deuteronomy 11:13-21. The passage cited from the twenty-eighth chapter of Deuteronomy is Deuteronomy 28:1-14. The remark that, no matter what, God will always restore the fortunes of Israel "and take them back in love" comes from Deuteronomy 30:3 in the new translation of the Jewish Publication Society (Philadelphia, 1985.) The passages from Deuteronomy cited are as follow: Deuteronomy 4:40 ("keep the commandments ... so that it be good for you and for your children after you"), 6:2 ("... so that you fear the Lord ... and so that you live a long life"), 7:12-15 ("... then God will love you and bless you and multiply you and bless the fruit of your womb and the fruit of your land, your new grain and wine and oil, the calving of your herd and the lambing of your flock ... you shall be blessed above all other peoples; there shall be no sterile male or female among you or among your livestock. The Lord will ward off from you all sickness ..."), 8:1 ("... so that you live and multiply and come to inherit the land ..."), 11:9 ("so that you live a long life in the land ..."), 12:28 ("... so that it be good for you and for your descendants forever ..."), 15:6 ("... for the Lord your God will bless you ... you shall lend to other nations, but you shall not borrow / you shall rule over many nations, but none shall rule over you"), 30:9 ("... and the Lord will grant you great prosperity in all your undertakings, (and also) in the fruit of your womb and the fruit of your animal(s' wombs) and the fruit of the land ...") and 30:16 ("... that you live and multiply and that the Lord your God bless you ....") The passage in which the text insists that the real reward Israel can expect in return for keeping its side of the covenant is God's help in driving out the indigenous peoples of Canaan is found at Exodus 34:11. The passage at the end of Leviticus listing the rewards Israel may hope to attain is found at Leviticus 26:3-13. The passage in which it is related that Moses saw the *temunah* of God when he experienced his prophetic visions is found at Numbers 12:8. The author of the sixty-third psalm used the prophetic word *hazah* to describe his experience of mystic communion with the godhead in the third verse of his poem. The reference to the eleventh psalm is to Psalm 11:7. The reference in the twenty-seventh psalm to gazing at the face of God is at Psalm 27:4. (References to the divine face and to the divine beauty are brought together at the end of the sixteenth psalm as well.) The passage in which the poet says openly that God responds from "His holy mountain" when the poet calls on Him is at Psalm 3:5. My reference to the forty-second psalm is to Psalm 42:3, reading *'ereh* for *'êra'eh* along with the Targum. (Cf. Exodus 23:15 and 17, and 34:20, 23 and 24, Deuteronomy 16:16 and 31:11, 1 Samuel 1:22 and Isaiah 1:12 for other passages about seeing God in which the massoretic reading offers a passive verb where the unpointed text would more logically be read as a *qal*, i.e. active, verb. That these shifts from active to passive verbs were intentional was already discussed by A. Geiger in his *Urschrift und Übersetzungen der Bibel*, 2nd edition [Frankfurt, 1928], pp. 237ff.) The passage from the 140th psalm is found at Psalm 140:14. My reference to the 111th psalm is to its first verse. The passage from the twenty-fourth psalm is found in its sixth verse, following the new JPS translation of the Hebrew *dor* as "circle", regarding which, see N. Sarna's note in his *On the Book of Psalms: Exploring the Prayers of Ancient Israel* (1993; rpt. New York, 1995), p. 243, note 115. Regarding the parallel structure of the Torah and the Psalter, cf. the passage from *Midrash Tehillim* 1:2, ed. Buber (Vilnius, 1891), p. 3: "Moses gave the five books of the Torah (*hamishah humshê torah*) to Israel and David gave the five books of the Psalter (*hamishah sefarim shebetehillim*) to Israel." The passage continues with a long list of ways in which Moses and David were parallel figures and cf. also the discussion of this point in Nahum Sarna's *On the Book of Psalms*, pp. 17-18. Sarna makes the point that the Chronicler specifically suggests that Moses and David were parallel figures twice, once at 2 Chronicles 8:13-14 and then again at 2 Chronicles 23:18. Furthermore, it seems at least reasonable to theorize that the division of the Psalter into 150 hymns is somehow connected to the old Palestinian division of the Torah into just that many lectionary readings. (Regarding this slightly obscure parallel, see Sarna's essay in the *Journal of Biblical Literature* 87(1968), pp. 100-106. The larger questions relating to the division of the Psalter into five books are discussed by M. Haran in the *Proceedings of the Israel National Academy of Sciences* 8:1(1989), pp. 1-32.) Other rabbinic texts suggest that the Torah was David's inspiration for composing the psalms, cf. the tradition preserved at *BT Berakhot* 3b in the name of Rav Ashi to the effect that David used to study Torah until midnight, then compose psalms until dawn. The references to Psalms 34 and 50 are to Psalms 34:5 and 50:3.

Chapter Two: The Chronicler gives the name of seven great-great-great-great-great-great-great-grandsons of Zerubbabel at 1 Chronicles 3:24 in a difficult passage that can bear interpretation in a variety of ways. (Note that the Book of Nehemiah, together with the Book of Ezra widely considered to be part of the Chronicler's larger opus, gives the name of the High Priest six generations after Jeshua, who was Zerubbabel's contemporary and partner in the governance of Judah at the end of the sixth century B.C.E. The priest's name, Jaddua, is given at Nehemiah 12:11.) On the precise date of the Chronicler, see Martin Noth, *The Chronicler's History* (trans. H.G.M. Williamson; Sheffield, 1987), pp. 69-73, Adam C. Welch, *The Work of the Chronicler: Its Purpose and Date* (London, 1939) and Peter Ackroyd, "The Age of the Chronicler," printed in a supplement to *Colloquium: The Australian and New Zealand Theological Review* (Auckland, 1970) and now reprinted in the author's *The Chronicler in His Age* (Sheffield, 1991: *Journal for the Study of the Old Testament*, supplementary vol. 101), pp. 8-86. Regarding the attribution of the psalms, the interested reader will wish to know that the eighty-eighth psalm is attributed both to Heman and to the sons of Korach and that the psalms attributed to Jeduthun also all have double attributions, psalms 39 and 62 to David and psalm 77 to Asaph. Also of interest is that psalms 62 and 77 both have superscriptions that read as though Jeduthun were the name of a musical instrument rather than the name of the composer of the song. (Regarding Jeduthun, see Rashi's comment to Psalm 1:1.) The ancient Greek translation of Scripture, the Septuagint, omits the attribution of Psalm 127 to Solomon and adds attributions of Psalm 137 to Haggai and Psalms 146, 147 and 148 to Haggai and Zachariah. The rabbis attributed psalms to Adam, Abraham and Melchizedek as well at *BT Baba Batra* 14b. Rashi explains (*ad loc.*) that they were thinking of the 139th psalm with respect to Adam, of the 110th psalm with respect to Melchizedek and, in that they took Ethan to be his cognomen, of the eighty-ninth psalm with respect to Abraham. Cf. the amplified parallel passage at *Shir Hashirim Rabbah* 4:4. The Chronicler does mention some of the sons of Korach by name (at 1 Chronicles 9:19 and 31 and at 12:7) but there is no reference to them being composers or singers of songs and neither does the author refer to them as seers or prophets. Nonetheless, the author does slip in a reference (at 2 Chronicles 29:11) to the Levites engaging in the offering of incense, precisely the ritual act that the Torah portrays as the one that brought about the final destruction of (the original) Korach and his followers. The musical guilds and the issues relating to them are discussed in detail by N. Sarna in his essay, "The Psalm Superscriptions and the Guilds" in *Studies in Jewish Religious and Intellectual History Presented to Alexander Altmann*, eds. Stein and Lowe (University of Alabama Press, 1979), pp. 281-300. On the general question of the Chronicler's attitude towards music and singing, see John W. Kleinig's *The Lord's Song: The Basis, Function and Significance of Choral Music in Chronicles* (Sheffield [U.K.], 1991=*Journal for the Study of the Old Testament*, Supplement vol. 156.) Regarding the 288 descendants of Asaph, Heman and Jeduthun, see Raymond Jacques Tournay, *Seeing and Hearing God with the Psalms: The Prophetic Liturgy of the Second Temple in Jerusalem* (=Journal of the Study of the Old Testament Supplement Series, no. 118; Sheffield [U.K.]: Sheffield Academic Press, 1991), p. 38, and also see below, chapter 12. The story of the seventy elders whom God invested with the spirit of prophecy is told in the eleventh chapter of Numbers. The story of Yahaziel is told at 2 Chronicles 20:14-19. The Chronicler remarks that it was David himself who selected Asaph, Heman and Jeduthun (and their descendants) to be the "trained singers" in the sanctuary at 1 Chronicles 25:7. (Regarding women singers in the Second Temple, cf. verses 5b-6: "God gave Heman fourteen sons and three daughters, all of whom were under the charge of their father for the singing in the House of Lord, to the accompaniment of cymbals, harps and lyres, for the service of the House of God by order of the king.") The reference to Solomon being wiser than Heman (and also than Ethan the Ezrahite, to whom the eighty-ninth psalm is attributed) is found at 1 Kings 5:11. Regarding the possible identification of Jeduthun and Ethan, cf. passages like 1 Chronicles 6:16-33 and 15:16-17, which present Asaph, Heman and Ethan as the eponymous heads of Israel's musical guilds, with passages like 1 Chronicles 16:37-43 and 25:1-7, where Jeduthun appears with the other two instead of Ethan. The tradition that the Levitical singers were appointed to their positions by David appears again in Chronicles at 2 Chronicles 35:15. The story of how David reported a prophetically received message to Solomon appears at 1 Chronicles 22:7-10. Note that the Chronicler reports twice (at 1 Chronicles 22:8 and 29:3) that David said that the word of God regarding his plan to build a permanent temple in Jerusalem had come directly to him, i.e. in a prophetic state of communion with the divine, while at 1 Chronicles 17:1-10, he echoes the story preserved in 2 Samuel 7:4 to the effect that this same information was specifically said to have been conveyed to David by the prophet Nathan. The passages linking the figures of David and Elijah appear at 1 Kings 18:37-38 and 1 Chronicles 21:26. The passage in which the poet uses the same verb used of Moses at Exodus 2:10 to describe himself being drawn out of the water is the seventeenth verse of the eighteenth psalm (2 Samuel 22:17.) The eighteenth psalm is attributed to David. The term *'ish ha'elohim* is used to refer to Moses at Deuteronomy 33:1, Joshua 14:6, Ezra 3:2, Psalm 90:1, 1 Chronicles 23:14 and 2 Chronicles 30:16. David is also called *'ish ha'elohim* at Nehemiah 12:24. The Chronicler's report that God appeared to David is found at 2 Chronicles 3:1, which may be compared to the story at 2 Samuel 24:17. The passage offering the last words of David in which he identifies himself (more or less) as a prophet of God appears at 2 Samuel 23:2. Note also the prophetic style of 2 Samuel 23:1, which may be compared easily to the opening style of the two of Balaam's prophetic speeches found at Numbers 24:3 and 15. The passage in which Solomon is heard to remark that God spoke "with his mouth" to David is found at 1 Kings 8:15. (Cf. the reference to God speaking "mouth to mouth" with Moses at Numbers 12:18.) The modern author who wrote that David's Biblical portrait is that of a prophet as much as of a king was A. Robert, writing in his essay "*La sens du mot Loi dans le Ps. cxix (vulg. cxviii),*" Revue Biblique 46(1937), p. 202. Many ancient authors would have agreed with this sentiment, cf. Josephus, *Jewish Antiquities* 6:166, the author of Luke-Acts at Acts 2:30 ("... but since [David] was a prophet ...") and 4:25

and even the author of the Qumran scroll called 11QPs^a, who wrote that "David, son of Jesse, was a wise man, a light like the light of the sun ... the Lord gave him an intelligent and enlightened spirit. He wrote 3600 psalms ... All this he expressed under prophetic inspiration, which was given to him on the part of the most High (trans. Tourney in Raymond Jacques Tournay, *Seeing and Hearing God with the Psalms*, p. 44, and cf. the translation of J.A. Anders in *The Dead Sea Psalms Scroll* [Ithaca (New York), 1967], p. 137.) The talmudic tradition about David's composition of the psalms while under the direct influence of God's presence in the world is found at *BT Pesaḥim* 117a. Saadia's opinion about David's status as a prophet is recorded in his first introduction to the Book of Psalms, printed in his commentary to the Psalter, trans. and ed. Y. Kafih (Jerusalem, 1966), p. 28, cf. the comments of Uriel Simon in his *'Arba' Gishot Lesêfer Tehillim Mêrav Sa'adiah Ga'on 'Ad R. 'Avraham 'Ibn 'Ezra* (Ramat-Gan, 1982), pp. 13-54. Saadia then goes on to demonstrate why the specific attribution of various poems within the Psalter to other people does not rule out taking the entire book as the prophetic output of David. (Cf. Rashi to Psalm 72:20.) The Talmudic tradition to the effect that David was the editor of the Psalter is preserved at *BT Baba Batra* 15a. Ibn Ezra writes about the prophetic nature of the Psalter in his introduction to the Psalms (printed in Simon, *'Arba' Gishot*, p. 248.) Regarding the Chronicler's connection of the Levitical singers of his own day with the psalmists and songsters of David's time, see D.L. Petersen in his *Late Israelite Poetry: Studies in Deutero-Prophetic Literature* (Missoula, 1977), p. 85. The Chronicler gives his "revised" version of 1 Kings 23:2 at 2 Ch 34:30. Regarding this passage, see Petersen, loc. cit. and also J. Myers in his Anchor Bible commentary to Chronicles, vol. 2 (Garden City, 1965), p. 208. The idea that the Levitical singers of the Second Temple period were the spiritual descendants of the prophets is also related somehow to the mysterious way the Chronicler lists the names of the sons of Heman at 1 Ch 25:4. The last nine names on the list appear to form the fragment of some forgotten psalm that could be translated to yield: "Have mercy on me, Lord, have mercy, (for) you are my God / I have glorified and magnified Your Help / Still afflicted, I spoke: Grant many visions." The translation is tentative in part. See P. Haupt, "*Die Psalmverse in I Chr 25,4*" in the *Zeitschrift für die alttestamentliche Wissenschaft* 34(1914), pp. 142-145 and H. Torczyner, "A Psalm by the Sons of Heman," *Journal of Biblical Literature* 68(1949), pp. 247-249, both of whom offer quite different translations and cf. D.L. Petersen, op. cit., p. 65. The question of whether the traditions connecting David with the invention of psalmody were themselves developed within the levitical guilds of post-exilic Jerusalem is discussed briefly by Alan M. Cooper in his essay, "The Life and Times of King David According to the Book of Psalms," pp. 129-130, printed in *The Poet and the Historian: Essays in Literary and Historical Biblical Criticism*, ed. Richard E. Friedman (Chico [California], 1983), pp. 117-132.

Chapter Three: The story of Saul's anointing and subsequent experiences at the tomb of Rachel, Alon Tabor and Givat Ha'elohim is related at 1 Samuel 10:1-13. Groups of ecstatic prophets are specifically said to have lived at Bethel and Jericho in the beginning of the second chapter of 2 Kings. Groups of prophets connected to the royal court are mentioned in Scriptural accounts of the court of King Ahab at 1 Kings 18 and 22. It isn't obvious to me whether the reference to the prophets of Jerusalem in the time of King Josiah at 2 Kings 23:2 is to a group of royal prophets or not. (The evidence of Jeremiah 26:7, 8 and 11 suggests that there was simply a settlement of prophets in Jerusalem during the reign of King Jehoiakim, Josiah's son. These, presumably, would be the same prophets mentioned in 2 Kings 23, cf. Lamentations 2:14.) The wives of Isaiah and Ezekiel are referred to at Isaiah 8:3 and Ezekiel 24:18 respectively. The husband of the prophetess Hulda is named at 2 Kings 22:14. The divine command forbidding Jeremiah to marry "in this place" (i.e. in Jerusalem on the eve of its destruction) is preserved at Jeremiah 16:2. Scripture uses the phrase "spirit of God" as a synonym for the charismatic force of an individual's personality at 1 Samuel 11:6 and as a synonym for mental wellbeing at 1 Samuel 16:14, where the text conveys the idea that Saul was slowly becoming mad by stating that "the spirit of the Lord had departed from [him] and an evil spirit from the Lord began to terrify him." The Bible speaks of the spirit of God coming over Samson at Judges 14:6 and Jephthah at Judges 11:29. The remark of Obadiah, steward of Ahab's palace, about the power of the divine spirit is preserved at 1 Kings 18:12. The comments of the prophets of Jericho to Elisha about the power of that same spirit are given at 2 Kings 2:16. The story about Elijah outrunning Ahab's chariot is given at 1 Kings 18:41-46. The various verbs used to describe the way in which the divine spirit possesses a prophet are found in the following places: fills him with strength, at Micah 3:8; falls on him, at Ezekiel 11:5; comes mightily onto him (Hebrew: *tzalah*), at 1 Samuel 10:6 and 10; envelops him (Hebrew: *lavash*), at 1 Chronicles 24:20; descended upon him and rested on him, at Numbers 11:25. The passage about Saul at Naioth from 1 Samuel 19 is given in the translation of the latest Jewish Publication Society Bible. The Biblical text that talks about Levites being unable to recognize their close relatives is at Deuteronomy 33:9.

Chapter Four: Ahab's remark about Michaihu ("For I loathe him...") is found at 1 Kings 22:8. The citation from the story of Michaihu and Kings Ahab and Jehoshafat is taken from 1 Kings 22:16-19. (The story presented at 1 Kings 22 can be compared with the version that appears in 2 Chronicles 18.) The Bible reports that God appeared to Solomon at 1 Kings 3:5 and 9:2-3, to which the parallel passage at 2 Chronicles 7:12 may be compared. The rather obscure sole reference in the Bible to God appearing to David is at 2 Chronicles 3:1 in a passage that has no parallel in the Book of Kings. Amos is heard to report his experience of visual communion with God at Amos 9:1. The story of Isaiah's prophetic investiture is told at Isaiah 6:1-13. The quotation from the first chapter of Ezekiel is taken from Ezekiel 1:26-28. Ezekiel refers to the divine glory again in the vision described in Ezekiel 10 (where he implies strongly, but stops just short of saying in so many words, that the image of the godhead in this particular vision was the same as the one he had in his inaugural prophetic experience on the banks of the Kebar) and then again in Ezekiel 43:1-6, where he makes that precise observation explicitly. The vision of God described by the author of the Book of Daniel is preserved at Daniel 7:9-11, to which may be compared the text at Daniel 10:5-7.

Chapter Five: The verse that begins "And lo, the Lord passed by ..." is 1 Kings 19:11. The verse "To whom can one compare God ..." is Isaiah 40:18. The Psalter is divided into five books as follows: Book 1: Psalms 1-41, Book 2: Psalms 42-72, Book 3: Psalms 73-89, Book 4: Psalms 90-106 and Book 5: Psalms 107-150.

Chapter Six: The story of King Uzziah's mystic lessons is preserved (all too briefly) at 2 Chronicles 26:5. (The Hebrew verb used is *darash.*) The reference in the twenty-seventh psalm to seeking God within the precincts of the Temple is found at Psalm 27:4. The reference to a sacred meal in the twenty-second psalm is at Psalm 22:27, cf. Psalm 34:11, where the satiety of the "Seekers of God" (one of the terms also used in Psalm 22) is contrasted with the hunger of their rivals. (On the other hand, the beginning of the forty-second psalm could be read to suggest that those who sought out communion with the divine face did so in a context of fasting from food and, especially, from drink. Perhaps the idea is that the actual experience of communion was preceded by a period of fasting, but completed in the context of feasting.) The references to seeking God in the context of joyful song are at Psalms 69:33 and 70:5. (The singing of long, repetitive hymns was also a feature of the mystic methodology of the merkavah mystics of the Talmudic and post-Talmudic periods. See the responsum of Hai Gaon published by B.M. Levin in his *'Otzar Hagge'onim* to *Ḥagigah* [Jerusalem, 1932], p. 13-15.) The opening verses of the 105th psalm also include references to intense joy and the singing of hymns in the specific context of seeking communion with the face of God. Psalm 4:7-8 also connects the idea of experiencing the light of God's face with the idea of joy. Cf. Psalm 16:11 and 21:7, where the concepts of joy and the face of God are also linked.) The reference to Jacob in the twenty-fourth psalm is at Psalm 24:6. (The reference in the Torah to Jacob at Peniel is at Genesis 32:30.) The rabbinic tradition about the number of poems in the Book of Psalms is preserved among the extra-Talmudic tractates at *Sofrim* 16:11, cf. *Midrash Tehillim* to Psalms 22:19 (ed. Buber, p. 190) and 104:2 (ed. cit., p. 439) and the related material preserved at *BT Berakhot* 9b-10a and *PT* Shabbat 16:1, 15c. (The tradition is also cited by the Tosafot at *BT Pesaḥim* 117a, s.v. *hakhi garsinan*, and is implied in the large number of rabbinic passages collected and presented by Buber in his notes to the passages from *Midrash Tehillim* mentioned above.) Scripture gives the patriarch Jacob's age at his death as 147 at Genesis 47:28. References to God hiding His face are found in the Psalter at Psalms 13:2, 27:9, 30:8, 44:25, 51:11 (where the psalmist anomalously sees the image as something positive, i.e. that God will agree to turn His face away from the poet's sins), 69:18, 88:15, 102:3, 104:29 and 143:7. References to the light of the divine face may be found in the eightieth psalm in verses 4, 8 and 17 (where the reference is to fire rather than light and the idea is that the light can become too intense [i.e. it can turn to fire] if the epiphany is left uncontrolled; cf. Ps 21:10) and 20. Cf. also Psalms 31:17, 44:4, 89:15-16, 105:5, 90:8 and 119:135. The *yesharim* are said to sit with the divine face at Psalm 140:14. The psalmist refers to rising at midnight to supplicate before the divine face at Psalm 119:58 and 62, presuming both verses to be referring to the same experience. The reference to the servants of God rising at midnight to supplicate in the Temple courtyard is at Psalm 134:1. The references in the Psalter to the various names the latter-day prophets gave themselves are as follows: humble ones: Psalm 69:33; seekers of God: Psalm 34:11; seekers of the divine face: Psalm 24:6 or Psalm 70:5; upright ones: Psalm 140:14; the pious (Hebrew: *ḥasidim*): Psalm 132:9, where the term is used as the counterpart of *kohanim* (cf. Deuteronomy 33:8, where the term *ḥasid* is specifically applied to the tribe of Levi); the God-fearers: Psalm 115:9-11 and 118:2-4, where the group, presumably the Levites, within the Temple population that aren't the Israelites or the priests are called God-fearers (but cf. Psalm 135:19-20, where the God-fearers and the Levites are mentioned separately and also Psalms 25:14 and 34:8, where the poets appear to be presuming that their readers will recognize their references); the righteous: Psalm 118:20, where the people who pass through the gate to (gaze on?) God are called the Righteous (*tzaddiqim*); the servants of God: Psalm 134:1 (cf. Psalm 113:1). The reference to the eighty-ninth psalm is to verse twenty, which recasts 2 Samuel 7:4 as a group experience directed not to the prophet Nathan (as in Samuel), but to a group called "the pious" (Hebrew: *ḥasidim*.) The poet pleads with God that He not take the holy spirit of prophecy from him at Psalm 51:13. The passage from the 108th psalm is Psalm 108:8 (=Psalm 60:8.) The psalmists use the verb *darash* to characterize their search for God in several different poems, e.g. Psalms 34:5 (cf. verse 11), 53:3 and 77:3. That the word refers specifically to the cultivation of prophetic communion with the divine realm is obvious from many Biblical passages, e.g. Genesis 25:22-23, Exodus 18:5, 1 Samuel 9:9, 1 Kings 22:8, 2 Kings 3:11, 8:8, 22:13 and 18, Jeremiah 21:2 and 37:7, Ezekiel 20: 1 and 3, 1 Chronicles 15:13 and 21:30 and 2 Chronicles 17:7 and 34:21. Examples of the inconsistent redactional traits of the Psalter and the Torah are Psalm 72:20 ("Here end the prayer of David son of Jesse") when dozens of psalms ascribed to David follow and Leviticus 26:46 ("These are the statutes, laws and *torot* that God...gave into the hand of Moses at Mount Sinai") when the very next verse introduces a section of text said (at Leviticus 27:34) to be constituted of different laws given by God to Moses at Mount Sinai. (Even if the latter verse was meant to refer to all of Leviticus, then the book still has two endings.) A certain general unwillingness to smooth over obvious textual problems is also characteristic of the final editors of both works, but the evidence of this willingness varies according to the genre of the passage. In the legal portions of the Torah, for example, we have laws that are in obvious contradiction with each other (like the laws regarding the specific animals that may be used for the paschal sacrifice at Exodus 12:5 and Deuteronomy 16:2), while in the narrative portions of Torah, we have details from different versions of the same story presented as though they were entirely consonant with each other (like the detail of what the Midianites did with Joseph once they kidnapped him presented at Genesis 37:28 and 36). In the Psalter, on the other hand, we have the phenomena of acrostic poems being presented with some of their letters missing, either one single letter (as in Psalm 145) or a much larger number (as in Psalms 9 and 10, which the Septuagint presents as one single poem and which are, in effect, one long acrostic hymn) and also of the same poem appearing as two different psalms, e.g. Psalms 14 and 53. Parallel passages within the Psalter are as follows: Psalm 14=Psalm 53; Psalm 70:2-6=Psalm 40:14-18; Psalm 108=Psalm 57:8-12 and 60:7-14. The five books of the Torah are Genesis, Exodus, Leviticus, Numbers and Deuteronomy. The five books of the Psalter are given above in the notes to chapter five. The five books of the so-called Deuteronomic History are Deuteronomy, Joshua, Judges, Samuel and Kings. The Book of Proverbs consists of five distinct collections of material: chapters 1-9, 10-24, 25-29, 30 and 31. The Book of Daniel may also be broken down into five constituent units, each of which begins with the formal dates that appear in the book at the beginnings of chapters one, two, seven, eight and ten. The scholar who feels that the first nine chapters of 1 Chronicles was originally a distinct textual unit that was added onto the larger part of the work at a secondary stage of the book's redaction is Adam C. Welch, whose arguments are set forth in his *Post-Exilic Judaism* (Edinburgh and London, 1935), pp. 185ff.

Chapter Seven: The story of how Isaiah wandered naked in the streets of old Jerusalem is preserved in the twentieth chapter of the Book of Isaiah. The story of Moses', Samuel's, Jeremiah's, Amos' and Ezekiel's prophetic investitures may be found at Exodus 3:1-4:23, 1

Samuel 3:1-14, Jeremiah 1:1-19, Amos 7:12-17 and Ezekiel 1-7 respectively. Scripture does not present an account of the destruction of the sanctuary at Shiloh, but refers to it at Psalms 78:60. That the ark was taken into battle against the Philistines from Shiloh (as recounted at 1 Samuel 4:3-5), but not returned there seven months later when the Philistines relinquished it (it went first to Beth Shemesh and then to Kiryat Yearim; cf. 1 Samuel 6:19-7:1) suggests, at least obliquely, that it was at this point that Shiloh was destroyed, cf. the evidence of Psalm 78:60 and of Jeremiah 7:12 and 14 and 26:6. The comment of the Biblical author to the effect that prophecy was not widespread in the time of Samuel is found at 1 Samuel 3:1. The observation that the term "prophet" replaced the earlier seer is found at 1 Samuel 9:9. The story about how young Saul set out to seek a seer (who turns out to be none other than Samuel) to help him find his father's lost asses is told in 1 Samuel 9. Scripture says that Joshua remained permanently ensconced in the prophetic sanctuary that Moses built outside the camp during the years Israel wandered in the desert at Exodus 33:11. The Bible says that Samuel slept "where the Ark of God was" at Shiloh at 1 Samuel 3:3. Abraham says *hinêni* to God at Genesis 22:1 and 11, as do Jacob at Genesis 46:2 and Moses at Exodus 3:4. The full story of how Samuel first came to hear the word of God is told at 1 Samuel 3:1-18. Regarding Samuel's omission of God's name when he follows Eli's instructions (as recounted at 1 Samuel 3:10), see the *ad locum* comments of Rashi and, especially, Radak. Scripture says explicitly that Samuel's experience at Shiloh was his very first prophetic experience at 1 Samuel 3:7. The reference to Eli judging Israel for forty years is at 1 Samuel 4:18.

Chapter Eight: *Kên Baqqodesh ḥazitikhah*: Psalm 63:3. The story of Ezra reading to the people from a book he called "the book of the *torah* of Moses" is told in the eighth chapter of Nehemiah. The reasons for doubting that this book is the book we know as *the* Torah are three: first, that it appears to have had no reference in it to the Day of Atonement since the people appear to have known of no holiday between the first day of the seventh month (when they had gathered to hear Ezra read) and the feast of Sukkot on the fifteenth of that same month despite the fact that our Torah (at Leviticus 16:29 and 23:27) specifically indicates that the Day of Atonement is to be observed on the tenth. Furthermore, the citation from the book preserved at Nehemiah 8:15 not only does not appear in our Torah at all but appears to contradict the simple meaning of Leviticus 23:40. Finally, the Temple tax described in Nehemiah 10:33-34 is set at one-third of a shekel, which is contrary to the law of our Torah at Exodus 30:11-16, where the tax is set at a half shekel. The story of the translation of the Torah into Greek in the days of King Ptolemy II Philadelphus of Egypt is told in detail in the ancient book called The Letter of Aristeas. Scholars have debated the details of the legend forever, but it seems likely that the mid-third century date, at least, is fairly accurate. The Torah speaks of the Levites as the servants of the priests at Numbers 3:9, 8:16 and 8:19, cf. the slightly obscured reference at 18:6. Regarding the word *netunim*, see the comments of Jacob Milgrom on Numbers 3:9 in his commentary on Numbers published by the Jewish Publication Society (Philadelphia, 1990), p. 17. The story of the rebellion of Korach is told in Numbers 16, cf. the note at Numbers 26:11 to the effect that the sons of Korach did not actually die when their father and his followers were killed. Psalms 42, 44, 45, 46, 47, 48, 49, 84, 85, 87 and 88 are attributed to the otherwise unidentified "sons of Korach". (Psalm 88 bears a double attribution: to the sons of Korach, but also to Heman the Ezrahite.) The Psalter mentions the suffering of the priests during the siege of Jerusalem at Psalm 78:64. The prediction that the priests will know God in messianic times is one way to translate the two references to the priesthood in the ninth and sixteenth verses of the 132nd psalm. The reference to the priests' beards (or rather to Aaron's) is at Psalm 133:2. The story of David's installation of the ark in a tent at Jerusalem is told by the Chronicler at 1 Chronicles 15 and 16, to which may be compared the account of the same event at 2 Samuel 6. The medieval commentators upon whose work I've relied principally are Rashi, Ibn Ezra and the Meiri, whose commentary was published by Joseph Hakohen in Jerusalem in 1936 and subsequently reprinted. (The medievals, of course, took the attribution of the psalm literally and presumed the sixty-third psalm to be an actual poem of David's. I'm trying to access the depth of their insight into the Biblical text without abandoning my sense of its actual history.) The story of David in the wilderness of Ziph is told in 1 Samuel 23-24 and then again, with changes and additions, in 1 Samuel 26. (That the story of David in the wilderness of Ziph was one that engaged the circles that produced the psalms is evident from the superscription of the fifty-fourth psalm.) The story of how God took the kingship away from the House of Saul and gave it to "one worthier than he" is told in 1 Samuel 15. One account of Saul sending men to kill David is found at 1 Samuel 19:1-7. Saul specifically calls David a *ben mavvet* at 1 Samuel 20:31. The comments of David's men as he approaches the defecating Saul are preserved at 1 Samuel 24:4. (I have told the story as it appears in the Bible with only a few slight changes.) The story of how David and Abishai ben Zeruiah sneaked into the king's camp at Givat Hahakhilah is found at 1 Samuel 26:1-25. The reference to the *tardêmah* of God that kept Saul's soldiers asleep as David and Abishai penetrated their camp is at 1 Samuel 26:12. The translation of the *'êmah ḥashêkhah gedolah* of Genesis 15:12 as "great, dark dread" appears in the translation of the text published by the Jewish Publication Society Bible. The author of the sixty-third psalm expresses his wish that his enemies would go to hell at Psalm 63:10. The reference to foxes eating their gutted bodies is at verse 11. The superscriptions to the 57th and 142nd psalms both make reference to the (or perhaps, an) incident in David's life that took place in a cave.

Chapter Nine: *'Esbe'ah Behaqitz Temunatekhah*: Psalm 17:15. There are dozens of texts in the Psalter that can be characterized either as personal or communal laments–poems in which the poet decries his personal fate or the fate of his nation. The most forceful personal laments are Psalms 6, 7, 9, 10, 28, 31, 36, 55, 57 and 64. The best known communal laments are Psalms 12, 14, 60, 85 and 126. All of these texts are discussed in detail by W.H. Bellinger Jr. in his *Psalmody and Prophecy* (Sheffield [U.K.], 1984 [=*Journal for the Study of the Old Testament*, Supplement Series, volume 27), pp. 32-77. The author of the seventeenth psalm asserts that his vindication will come from God in the second verse of his poem, following the translation of the Hebrew *mishpat* in the 1985 Jewish Publication Society Bible. The reference to the poet's enemy being like a lion in ambush is found at verse 12 and the call to God to bring about his enemy's downfall is at verse 13. The poet's assertion that God will speak to him is found at verse 6. The remark that God spoke to Moses "mouth to mouth" is found at Numbers 12:8. There are references to God speaking to Moses "face to face" at Exodus 33:11 and at Deuteronomy 34:10. The reference to God speaking to Moses "as one man speaks to another" may also be found at Exodus 33:11. The word *temunah* appears in the Ten Commandments at Exodus 20:4 and Deuteronomy 5:8. Moses notes that the Israelites' experience of

God at Sinai was strictly aural and not at all visual at Deuteronomy 4:12. (He reiterates this point a few lines later at verse 15.) The text in Numbers 12 seems to be using *temunah* and *mar'eh* ("vision") as referring to distinctly different experiences of the divine, but cf. Job 4:16, where they are used as parallel terms. Scripture notes that Moses covered his face when he realized that he was about to behold God at the burning bush at Exodus 3:6. The remark to the effect that no human being can see God and live is found at Exodus 33:20. The reference to vomiting after eating a surfeit of honey is at Proverbs 25:16. The author of the seventeenth psalm refers to having enough wealth to leave behind a bequest to one's children in verse 14 of his poem. The story of how David arranged for Uriah's death and an account the aftermath of that deed are found in 2 Samuel 11 and 12. Bathsheba's note ("I'm pregnant") is cited at 2 Samuel 11:5. The account of how Absalom slept with his father's concubines is told at the end of 2 Samuel 16. Radak, in his comment to verse 2, connects the composition of the seventeenth psalm to the incident involving Uriah and Bathsheba, as does Sforno. Rashi assigns the composition of the psalm to the period immediately following that incident in his comment to Psalm 17:11. We can be certain that the story of David and Bathsheba played a role in the psalmists' thinking from the beginning of the fifty-first psalm, where it is specifically noted that that poem was written by David as a response to Nathan's intervention in the matter. Furthermore, it could certainly also be the case that the more than slightly obscure references to the death of a child that appear, if they are really there, in the superscriptions to the ninth and forty-sixth psalms (the latter even less obviously than the former) might well refer to this incident as well.

Chapter Ten: *'Aḥat Sha'alti*: Psalm 27:4. The epigraph is from act 5, scene 2, of Racine's play, *Athaliah*, in the translation of Kenneth Muir as published by Hill and Wang (New York, 1960), p. 283. (The French is: ... *de David un trésor est resté ... c'était des tristes Juifs l'espérence dernière.*) The references in the opening paragraph to the twenty-seventh psalm are as follows: evil men assailed the poet: verse 2; villains tried to devour his flesh: verse 2; armies besieged him: verse 3; he lived in an ongoing state of war: verse 3; he experienced evil days: verse 5; he was denounced in court by false witnesses whose testimony inspired violence against him: verse 12; he was under constant surveillance: verse 11. (The verbal system of classical

Hebrew makes it difficult in most of these instances to decide whether the poet was referring to repeated or single incidents he had experienced.) The comment of Sforno is cited by A.Y. Lebanon in his 1969 edition of the psalms called *Yalqut La'anaqim*. The Meiri's comment appears as his introduction to Psalm 27, ed. Hakohen (Jerusalem, 1936), p. 60. Ibn Ezra discusses the origin of the twenty-seventh psalm in his comment to Psalm 27:4, cf. his comment to Psalm 110:1. Although it is clear from the context they were executed, the precise nature of the fate the sons and grandsons of Saul met at the hands of the Gibeonites rests on the correct interpretation of the Hebrew word *vayyoqi'um* at 2 Samuel 21:9, a term variously translated as referring to impalement, exposition (i.e. of their bodies), crucifixion or some other form of solemn execution. (Cf. the brief summary in the Brown, Driver and Briggs lexicon (1907; rpt. Oxford, 1972), s.v. *yaqa'*, p. 429.) The assumption that Ishbibenob (whose name may simply mean Ishbi of Nob, cf. the comment of Radak *ad loc.*) was a giant is based on Radak's interpretation of the word *rafah* at 2 Samuel 21:16. The men of David are cited as declaring that their king shall "no longer go into battle with them" at 2 Samuel 21:17. The story of how Jehu assassinated the kings of Judah and Israel and came to the throne after being anointed king of Israel by a disciple of Elisha is told in 2 Kings 9 and 10, cf. 1 Kings 19:16. The story of the murderous Athaliah and how her stepdaughter Jehosheba saved the baby Joash (also called Jehoash in Scripture) is told in 2 Kings 11. The connection between the twenty-seventh psalm and the story of Joash and Jehosheba is preserved in the midrashic *Seder Olam Rabbah*, chapter 18, a passage to which Rashi makes reference in his comment to Psalm 27:5. Jehosheba is called Jehoshabeath at 2 Chronicles 22:11, where it is mentioned that she was the wife of the High Priest Jehoiada. The Torah uses the Hebrew verb *yehezu* at Exodus 24:11 to denote the experience of gazing on God. Following the suggestion of David Altschuler in his *Metzuddat Tziyyon* commentary to the Book of Kings (to 2 Kings 16:15), I have translated the word *levaqqêr* at Psalm 27:4 as "to tarry" in accordance with the clear, if unusual, meaning of the word at Leviticus 13:36. It is also possible that the verb in 2 Kings 16 refers to some specific cultic act, a point I first found made in Helmer Ringgren's *The Faith of the Psalmists* (Philadelphia, 1963), pp. 3ff. A verbal form of the word used to describe the beauty of God at Psalm 27:4 is used to describe the beauty of the Shulamith at Song of Songs 7:7.

Jeremiah uses the Hebrew word *hêkhal* to refer to the Jerusalem Temple at Jeremiah 7:4, which usage is mirrored dozens of times through the other Biblical books, especially the Book of Kings and Ezekiel. (That same word is used to denote the Temple in Jerusalem elsewhere in the Psalter as well, e.g. at Psalm 5:8, 79:1 or 138:2.) The line about the poet having been abandoned by his father and mother is Psalm 27:10. The words of the poet who wrote that God is especially close to the broken-hearted are preserved at Psalm 34:19. For an utterly different, entirely non-mystical appreciation of Psalm 27:4, the reader may consult Helmer Ringgren's book mentioned just above or Claus Westermann's *The Living Psalms* (trans. J.R. Porter; Grand Rapids, 1989), pp. 146-149.

Chapter Eleven: *Yêshvu Yesharim 'Et Panekhah*: Psalm 140:14. The reference to people laying snares and traps for the author of the 140th psalm is in verse 6 of his poem. The reference to the evil having tongues like serpents is in verse 4, as is the remark about the author's enemies having spider poison dripping from their lips. The remark about the poet's enemies having hearts full of evil schemes as they plot war against him all day long is found in the third verse of the poem. Ibn Ezra's sense of the specific circumstances of David's life the poet is trying to capture is found in his comment to verse 2. The story of David at the shrine of Nob is told in 1 Samuel 21. What exactly the ephod was behind which Ahimelech had stored Goliath's sword is unclear. See the brief discussion in the Brown, Driver and Briggs lexicon, s.v. *'êfod*, p. 65. "It's the best sword" is the Hebrew *'ên kamoha* at 1 Samuel 21:10. Doeg is called *'abir haro'im* 1 Samuel 21:8, cf. the comments of Rashi and Radak *ad locum*. The theories of Radak and the Rid regarding the reasons for which Doeg was hanging around Nob in the first place are found in their comments to 1 Samuel 21:8. The account of how Saul had the men, women and children of Nob killed is preserved at 1 Samuel 21:16-19. The reference to David accepting ultimate responsibility for the slaughter is at 1 Samuel 22:22. Levites are specifically called "servants of God" at Psalm 134:1, assuming that the poet is referring to the Levites who stood on sentry duty in the Temple, as discussed in 1 Chronicles 23. That the story of Doeg was of special interest to the authors of the poems that make up our Psalter is obvious from the superscription to the fifty-second psalm, which notes that it was composed "when Doeg the Edomite came and told Saul that David had been to the house of Ahimelech."

Chapter Twelve: *Yoshêv Hakkeruvim Hofi'ah*: Psalm 80:2. It is noted that David and his generals chose Asaph and his colleagues to become prophet/singers at 1 Chronicles 25:1. Asaph's sons are named at 1 Chronicles 25:2. Asaph is designated "a royal prophet" in the same verse. The number of descendants of Asaph, Heman and Jeduthun is given at 1 Chronicles 25:7. The story of how Moses ordained the first raft of public prophets is told at Numbers 11:16-30. The references to the prophets "singing in the House of the Lord" is at 1 Chronicles 25:6. The phrase "raising a horn as a seer" is found at 1 Chronicles 25:5. The name of Asaph's father is given at 1 Chronicles 6:24 and 15:17. The reference to Asaph playing a bronze cymbal when David first brought the Ark of the Law to Jerusalem is at 1 Chronicles 15:19, cf. 1 Chronicles 6:16-33 and 16:37. Scripture notes that 128 descendants of Asaph returned from exile in Babylon at Ezra 2:41 and Nehemiah 7:44. (Cf. the list preserved at Nehemiah 11:17, in which it is noted that a descendant of Jeduthun apparently appeared among the Levites in Jerusalem later on, cf. 1 Chronicles 9:15-16.) The remark to the effect that Hezekiah and his officers ordered the Levites to sing songs by David and Asaph during the rededication of the Temple in the first year of Hezekiah's reign is preserved at 2 Chronicles 29:30, which is also where David's name is linked specifically to Asaph's. Nehemiah notes that the musical organization of the Temple was already in place "in the days of David and Asaph" at Nehemiah 12:46. The twelve psalms assigned to Asaph are Psalms 50 and 73-83. The poet wrote that we can only see light in the light of God at Psalm 36:10, cf. the remark at Psalm 112:4 to the effect that God shines a light in the darkness for the upright (Hebrew: *yesharim*). References to the text of the eightieth psalm are as follow: the poet drinks his own tears: verse 6; his neighbours hate him: verse 7; his enemies treat him with contempt: verse 7; Israel is a vine once tended by God: verse 9; wild pigs feed on the vine: verse 14. The description of the cherubim that graced the ark in the Tabernacle is given at Exodus 25:18-22. The rabbinic tradition to the effect that the cherubs were depicted in amorous embrace is preserved at *BT Yoma* 54a-b.

Chapter Thirteen: *Mitziyyon 'Elohim Hofi'a*: Psalm 50:3. References from the fiftieth psalm are as follow: God is bored with sacrifice: verses 9-10; God doesn't hunger or thirst: verse 12; God doesn't eat the sacrificial flesh or drink the blood of libation: verse 13; God wishes to be sought, not merely worshipped: verse 15; the priests are evil men: verse 16; God can't recall the origin of the priests' right to teach Torah: verse 16; the priests are friendly with thieves and adulterers: verse 18; the priests are slanderers: verses 19-20; God looks with favour on the *todah*: verse 23. The rules of the *todah* sacrifice are given at Leviticus 7:11-21. The rules for the larger category of well-being sacrifice (Hebrew: *shelamim*, singular form: *shelem*, cf. Amos 5:22 and the discussion in George Wolf's *Some Lexicographical Comments on the Hebrew Bible* [New York, 1990], p. 140) are found at Leviticus 7:11-38.) The *todah* sacrifice is mentioned in a number of different passages in the Psalter, e.g. Psalms 50:23 or 69:31. The long passage from Nehemiah's diary is taken from Nehemiah 12:27-43, *passim*. The author who has written about the Jerusalem Temple as a "sanctuary of silence" is Israel Knohl in his *The Sanctuary of Silence: The Priestly Torah and the Holiness School* (trans. Feldman and Rodman; Minneapolis, 1995.) Scripture lists the Levites in charge of singing hymns of praise and thanksgiving at Nehemiah 12:24, cf. verse 28, reading the word *lêvi* after *benê* with at least one ancient manuscript of the Septuagint, cf. the comment of J. Myers in his commentary to Nehemiah in the Anchor Bible Series (Garden City [New York], 1965), p. 200. The text at Nehemiah 12:35 notes that the priests were playing trumpets, which I suppose must mean that it was the Levites who were singing. See Myers' table of participants in the ceremony, op. cit., p. 204. The passage from the fifty-first psalm to which I refer is Psalm 51:18-21, the beginning of which sounds to me like a paraphrase of Hosea 6:6. The passage from the fortieth psalm is Psalm 40:7, which echoes the almost amazingly iconoclastic sentiments of Jeremiah 7:22-23.

Chapter Fourteen: *'Anêni* appears many times in the Psalter, e.g. at Psalms 4:2, 13:4, 27:7, 55:3, 60:7 (reading the text according to the suggested massoretic *qeri* reading), 69:14,17 and 18, 86:1, 102:3, 108:7, 119:145, cf. Psalm 20:10, 65:6, 91:14, 119:26 and 138:3. (The plural form *'anênu* ["Answer us!"] appears in the Psalter at 60:7 according to the uncorrected massoretic text.) The story of confrontation between Elijah and the prophets of Baal at Mount Carmel is told in 1 Kings 18. The prophets cry *'anênu* and Elijah cries out *'anêni* at verses 26 and 37 respectively. Psalms 120-134 are designated "songs of the steps" in the Psalter. The rabbinic traditions about the "songs of the steps" are preserved in the *Mishnah* at Sukkah 5:4 and Middot 2:5 and in the Talmud at *BT Sukkah* 53a, cf. the comments of Rashi and Ibn Ezra to Psalm 120:1. The reference to the twelfth psalm is to Psalm 12:6. The oracular portion of the seventy-fifth psalm begins with verse 3. The words "O God, do not be silent, do not hold aloof, do not be quiet, O God" come from Psalm 83:2.

Chapter Fifteen: *Zeh Hasha'ar Lashem*: Psalm 118:20. The epigraph from Kafka is from his story "*Vor Dem Gesetz*". Radak refers to the rabbinical approach to this psalm in his comment to the first verse of the poem. References to the text of the 118th psalm are as follows: the author is in distress: verse 5; surrounded on all sides: verse 10-11; enemies are like bees: verse 12; he can no more trust in human beings: verse 8; he even mistrusts people of renown: verse 9; God answered him and brought him relief: verse 5; the experience was torture, but in the end God did not hand him over to death: verse 18. The verse *yasar* is used of torture by whip and scorpion at 1 Kings 12:11 and 14. Reference is made to the *tzaddiqim* in the Psalms at Psalms 1:5-6; 32:11; 33:1; 34:16; 37:17, 29 and 39; 52:8; 68:4; 69:29; 97:12; 118:15 and 20; 125:3; 140:14; 142:8 and 146:8. Reference is made to individuals called *tzaddiqim* at Psalms 37:12, 16 and 32; 55:23; 58:12 and 97:11. As discussed above, the end of the 140th psalm actually says that the *yesharim* ("the upright") will dwell with the face of God, but the structure of the verse implies that the *yesharim* and the *tzaddiqim* are the same people. The verse I've cited from the 125th psalm is verse 3, translated with a bit of poetic licence. The story of Jacob's vision at Bethel is told in Genesis 28:10-19. The reference to Jacob in the twenty-fourth psalm is in verse 6, cf. the material collected above in the notes to chapter 6 relating to the connection between Jacob's age at his death and the number of psalms in the Psalter.

Chapter Sixteen: *Sefat Lo Yada'ti 'Eshma'*: Psalm 81:6. The phrase *'am segulah* ("a treasured people") appears in the Torah at Deuteronomy 7:6, 14:2 and 26:18, cf. Malachi 3:17, 1 Chronicles 29:3 and Psalm 135:4. The expression *goy qadosh* ("a holy people") appear in the Torah at Exodus 19:6, cf. Leviticus 11:44-45 and 19:2 and Numbers 16:3 among many other examples of the Israelite nation either being called or exhorted to become *qadosh*. The

Chronicler's version of Josiah's prayer is given at 2 Chronicles 35:3-6. The specific reference to the Levites as being holy is in verse 3. The references to the twelfth and thirty-second psalms are to Psalms 12:6 and 32:9 respectively, cf. the comment of Rashi to Psalm 32:9, which fleshes out the meaning of the reference to donkeys and mules a bit more clearly. The references to Shechem and the valley of Sukkot appears twice in the Psalter, once at Psalm 60:8 and then again at Psalm 108:8. (Since the 108th psalm is made up of pieces of two others psalms, I assume that the original setting for the oracle about Shechem must have been the sixtieth psalm.) The references to Babylon and Rahab in the eighty-seventh psalm are in verse four. The reference in the seventy-fifth psalm to God judging the world equitably (Hebrew: *mêsharim*) is in the third verse of the poem. The verse about the tongues of the psalmists' dogs lapping up their enemies' blood is found at Psalm 68:24. (The text is difficult and my translation, based on the latest translation of the Jewish Publication Society, ignores the traditional massoretic punctuation of the verse.) The reference to the enemies of the author's lord becoming his footstool is at Psalm 110:1. (The rabbinic tradition connects this psalm with Abraham as he prepared to do battle with King Chedorlaomer of Elam and his allies, cf. the comments of Rashi to verses 1 and 7, Ibn Ezra to verse 1 and the comments of Radak to verse 1. The Meiri takes the entire psalm to be discussing the Messiah, an ironic approach given the spin on the first verse of the psalm developed within Christian tradition, cf., e.g., the use made of the psalm in the New Testament at Mark 12:35-37 (and parallels at Matthew 22:41-46 and Luke 20:41-44.) The admonition not to be stubborn in the face of the tangible evidence of divine power is at Psalm 95:8-9. The references to being supportive of the poor and generous to orphans are at Psalm 82:3-4 in a passage that appears to have resulted from the poet's perception that he heard God speaking not precisely to him, but to some celestial gathering of the divine underlings who administer justice in the world. The reference to God judging each individual according to that person's own deeds is at Psalm 62:13 in a passage specifically labelled (in verse 12) as an oracle. The psalmist notes that he was specifically warned away from foolishness (Hebrew: *kislah*) at Psalm 85:9. References to the eighty-first psalm are as follow: the night of the new moon masking the proceedings under a blanket of semi-darkness: verse 4; a hymn accompanied by drum and harp: verse 3; the Deity is invoked as the God of Jacob: verse 1 (the connection between Jacob and the seekers of the God's face is at Psalm 24:6); a blast on the *shofar* sounds: verse 4 (the *shofar* at Sinai: Exodus 19:19); the poet hears a language he never knew to exist: verse 6 (the reference to the language of truth in the Book of Proverbs is at Proverbs 12:19); the quest for God is as old as the Exodus: verses 4-5; the setting aside of ritual paraphernalia: verse 7; God says that he will answer in thundering secrecy: verse 8 (Elijah's voice of silence: 1 Kings 19:12); the experience of hearing the word of God is a test of the prophet's mettle: verse 8 (the reference to Meribah may be read in light of the narrative at Exodus 17:1-7); God will fill the prophet's mouth with prophecy: verse 11; Israel must obey God: verse 9; Israel must worship no alien gods: verse 10; Israel must recognize God as the Master of History: verse 11; Israel must abandon its wilful ways: verse 12; God will crush the enemies of Israel: verse 15; the enemies of Israel will cower before God: verse 16 (taking the Hebrew *yikhaḥashu-lo* in light of Psalms 18:45 and 66:3 as does the new Jewish Publication Society translation); honey from the rock: verse 17.

Epilogue: *Lo' Navi 'Anokhi*: Amos 7:14. The epigraph is taken from Amos 5:6 (=5:4). The texts relating to the prophetic *'ohel mo'êd* cited in this chapter are Exodus 33:7-11, Numbers 11:16-29, Numbers 12:4-8 and Deuteronomy 31:14-15. The phrase denoting "all those who seek God" at Exodus 33:7 is the Hebrew *kol mevaqqêsh hashem*. The words *'ohel* or *'ohel mo'ed* are used regularly to denote the *mishkan*, as, e.g. at Leviticus 8:1-3 ("The Lord spoke to Moses, saying: Take Aaron along with his sons and the vestments, the anointing oil, the bull of sin offering, the two rams and the basket of unleavened bread and assemble the whole community at the entrance of the *'ohel mo'ed.*") Sometimes the text creates an odd conflate of terms, as, e.g., at Exodus 39:32, where the text refers to the *mishkan* of the *'ohel mo'ed*, or at Exodus 39:40, where the text simply tacks a reference to the *'ohel mo'ed* onto an otherwise perfectly comprehensible statement about the *mishkan*. In Exodus 40, the word *'ohel* is used repeatedly to denote the Tabernacle within the camp, e.g., at Exodus 40:6 ("You shall place the altar of burnt offering before the entrance of the Tabernacle of the *'ohel mo'ed*"), but the final five verses show clearly how the prophetic tent was turned into the priestly tabernacle - even its pillar of cloud (which indicates the communicative presence of the Deity in Exodus 33) has been recast as a kind of divinely inspired weather vane leading the Israelites off in the right direction and at the precisely most auspicious time for them to pursue their desert wandering. Other passages are equally tantalizing. When Leviticus itself opens with God instructing Moses (not Aaron!) about the specific ins and outs of sacrificial law "from (i.e. from within) the *'ohel mo'ed*", the text could certainly mean that God spoke to Moses at the tent outside the camp. The traditional explanation that God spoke from between the wings of the golden cherubs mounted atop the *kapporet* (i.e. the so-called "mercy-seat") within the priestly sanctuary derives directly from Exodus 25:22, but the only place in Scripture where Moses is actually said to have entered the Sanctuary to hear the divine voice issue forth is Numbers 7:89. The stories in which Moses acts like a prophet are located as follows: the story of the daughters of Zelophehad at Numbers 27:5, the story of the man who gathered sticks on the Sabbath at Numbers 15:34, the story of the blasphemer at Leviticus 24:12 and the story of the people who were unsure how to proceed because they were in a state of impurity during the celebration of Passover at Numbers 9:8. The Biblical tradition to the effect that even Aaron (let alone the non-priest Moses) may not enter the innermost sanctum of the sanctuary whenever he wishes is preserved at Leviticus 16:2. Scripture mentions the roles of Bezalel and Oholiab at Exodus 35:30-36:1. The Levites are called the slaves of the priests at Numbers 3:9, 8:16 and 8:19; see above, chapter 8. (For a traditional attempt to coordinate the traditions about the two tents without having to insist that they were actually the same place, see Rashi's comments to Exodus 33:11.) References to worries about enemies in the Psalter are as follow: overwhelmed by hostile forces: Psalm 42:11; foes too many to count: Psalm 3:2; enemies seeking to kill: Psalm 40:15. Scripture refers to Aaron as Moses' brother, the Levite, at Exodus 4:14. The poet's reference to how lovely it would be for brethren to sit down together is at Psalm 133:1. The phrase "Torah of God" appears in the Bible at Joshua 24:26, Ezra 7:10, Nehemiah 8:18, 9:3 and 10:29, 1 Chronicles 22:12 and 2 Chronicles 12:1, 17:9 and 34:14. The reference to serving God by abandoning the Torah is at Psalm 119:126. The reference to there being a *torah* within the psalmist's bowels is at Psalm 40:9. The reference to the private scroll is at verse 8 of that same poem. Ezekiel's account of the private scroll that filled up his own bowels is preserved at Ezekiel 3:1-3. Jeremiah writes about his intestines at Jeremiah 4:19. The story of Amos and

Amaziah is told at Amos 7:10-17. The prophet's remark that he is neither a *navi'* nor a *ben navi'* is slightly ambiguous and I have translated it differently in different contexts, taking the later expression both to denote non-membership in the prophetic guild called the *benê nevi'im* and, somewhat more literally, to mean that Amos was not the biological son of a prophet. The words "to come to the temple and to gaze on the beauty of the divine form" are a paraphrase of Psalm 27:4 (see above, chapter 10.) The words *bekhol lêv yidreshuhu* come from the second verse of the 119th psalm.

About the Author

Martin Samuel Cohen was born and grew up in New York City, but currently lives with his wife and three children in Richmond, British Columbia where he is the rabbi of the Beth Tikvah Congregation. In addition to his rabbinic ordination, he has earned a Ph.D. in the history of ancient Judaism and has been a post-doctoral fellow at the Hebrew University of Jerusalem and at Harvard University. His critically acclaimed first novel, *The Truth about Marvin Kalish*, was published in 1992 and was followed in 1996 by *Light from Dead Stars*. A new novel, *The Sword of Goliath*, will be released in the spring of 1998. He is also the author of two previous collections of essays, *Travels on the Private Zodiac: Reflections on Jewish Life, Ritual, and Spirituality* (1995) and *In Search of Wholeness: The Pursuit of Spiritual Integrity in a Delusional World* (1996), both published by Moonstone Press. In addition to his work as rabbi and author, Martin Samuel Cohen also serves as chairman of the Publications Committee of the Rabbinical Assembly.